Former prisoners at Dachau celebrate on April 30, 1945,
the day after the camp's liberation. (NARA)

Buchenwald, Germany, April 11, 1945. (NARA)

Germans rebury the corpses of 200 slave laborers found
near Bergen-Belsen. Lüneburg, Germany, October 3, 1945.

The courtroom at the International Military Tribunal.
Nuremberg, Germany, 1945. (IWM)

Displaced persons awaiting transport to trains
bound for their homes in the Netherlands, Belgium, and
France. Hanover, Germany, May 9, 1945. (NARA)

LIBERATION 1945

UNITED STATES HOLOCAUST MEMORIAL MUSEUM
WASHINGTON, DC

Photo credits are abbreviated as:

IWM: Imperial War Museum, London, U.K.

NARA: Still Picture Branch, National Archives and Records
           Administration, College Park, Maryland

USHMM: United States Holocaust Memorial Museum Photo
           Archive, Washington, D.C.

Published on the occasion of the exhibition
Liberation 1945, held at the
United States Holocaust Memorial Museum,
Washington, D.C.
May 9, 1995 – January 7, 1996

©1995 United States Holocaust Memorial Council

Library of Congress Catalog Card Number: 94-60762

ISBN: 0-89604-701-6

Project Director: Stephen Goodell
General Editor: Susan D. Bachrach
Editorial Assistance: Alice Greenwald
Photo Research: Andrew A. Campana
Research Assistance: Paul F. Rose
Copy Editor: Edward J. Phillips

Design: Marc Zaref Design, New York, NY
Photography: Edward Owen, Alex Jameson (artifacts);
    Morris Lane (cover flags)
Printing: Herlin Press, West Haven, CT

Cover: Photograph taken at Ebensee on May 7, 1945 (NARA),
against flags of some of the United States Army divisions that
liberated concentration camps in Europe in 1945

TABLE OF CONTENTS

V-E Day celebration, touched off by an early report of
Germany's unconditional surrender. Chicago, May 7, 1945.
(Bettmann Archive, New York)

Leonard Dinnerstein

The Holocaust is an unimaginable series of events. Even now, fifty years after the liberation of the concentration camps, it is impossible to discuss adequately the bestiality and inhumanity of the Nazis in their treatment of those whom they considered the *Untermenschen* (subhumans) of the world.

Jews were the primary victims—six million were murdered in a systematic genocidal program carried out under the cover of World War II; Gypsies, the handicapped, and Poles were also targeted for destruction or decimation for racial, ethnic, or national reasons. Millions more, including homosexuals, Jehovah's Witnesses, Soviet prisoners of war, and political dissidents, also suffered grievous oppression and death under German tyranny between 1933 and 1945.

This account focuses on the spring of 1945, when the Allied advance into Germany uncovered numerous concentration camps, and later, when the Allied occupying forces established assembly centers to temporarily house survivors awaiting new destinations.

Although joyous V-E (Victory in Europe) Day celebrations from Chicago to London and Moscow marked Germany's unconditional surrender on May 8, 1945, and the end of the war in Europe, the liberation of the camps was not a one-dimensional, celebratory event. Rather, it was a situation fraught with tragedies and contradictions.

For many survivors, liberation was both a release from terror and the beginning of a new phase of anomie and homelessness. For the liberating troops, it brought the shock of witnessing horrible atrocities and the challenges of a massive relief effort. In the liberated camps, Allied soldiers encountered a new set of enemies, including rampant disease and hunger. Despite the relief teams' valiant efforts, thousands of newly freed prisoners died inside the liberated camps. After the first few weeks of liberation, the Allies faced an additional problem as they struggled to deal with thousands of angry and bewildered survivors who had become displaced persons waiting word on their next destination.

PROLOGUE: LIBERATIONS IN THE EAST

For many of us, concentration camps and death camps are synonymous terms, but during World War II they were not. Nazi centers for genocide existed in occupied Poland: Auschwitz-Birkenau, Chelmno, Treblinka, Sobibor, Majdanek, and Belzec. In the West, the Allied armies liberated concentration camps like Dachau, Buchenwald, and Bergen-Belsen, where many atrocities occurred but within whose confines the primary goal had been to provide slave labor to aid the German economy and war effort.

One of Hitler's early policies, inaugurated in 1933 with the establishment of the first concentration camp at Dachau, near the city of Munich, was to set up concentration camps to detain political prisoners and individuals the German state deemed "undesirables." After the war broke out, the Nazi camp system spread across German-occupied Europe and evolved into centers of forced labor and/or extermination. Rumors abounded about the horrors that existed in these centers, such as brutal beatings, starvation, torture, and "medical experimentation." By 1942, reports also indicated that at some camps, systematic killing of the inmates took place. Remembering the false atrocity stories of World War I, many people considered the stories exaggerations or simply refused to believe anything so horrific.

When the Soviet army liberated Majdanek in July 1944 and Auschwitz-Birkenau six months later, they discovered, to their horror, that the rumored atrocities were true. At Majdanek, one of the six Nazi killing centers located in occupied Poland, the Soviets found gas chambers, crematoria, and 700 remaining prisoners. On January 27, 1945, when the Red Army liberated Auschwitz-Birkenau, the largest of the killing centers, they found only 7,000 sick prisoners alive. At Auschwitz the Germans had murdered an estimated 1 million Jews and another hundred thousand Poles, Roma and Sinti (Gypsies), Soviet prisoners of war, and others.

With the rapid advance of the Red Army, the Germans moved camp populations from the east to what remained of the Greater Reich. Prisoners were to be used as forced labor for the war effort. SS personnel evacuated inmates by foot across ice and snow or in unheated or open railroad cars and shot thousands too weak to keep up.

The survivors of these "death marches" flooded the western concentration camps. These western camps had not been intended as killing centers for mass murders, although thousands perished in them from 1933 to 1945 as a result of executions and brutal treatment. In the spring of 1945, however, as the Nazi regime collapsed and Allied bombing disrupted supply lines for fuel, food, and water, hundreds died every day from malnutrition, exposure, and disease in the overcrowded camps.

Although the atrocities at Majdanek and Auschwitz were reported in the western press, the depth of Nazi brutality was not fully appreciated until the liberation of concentration camps in Germany and Austria by Anglo-American forces in April and May 1945.

Survivors at Auschwitz, after January 26, 1945.
(Central Archives of the October Revolution, Moscow)

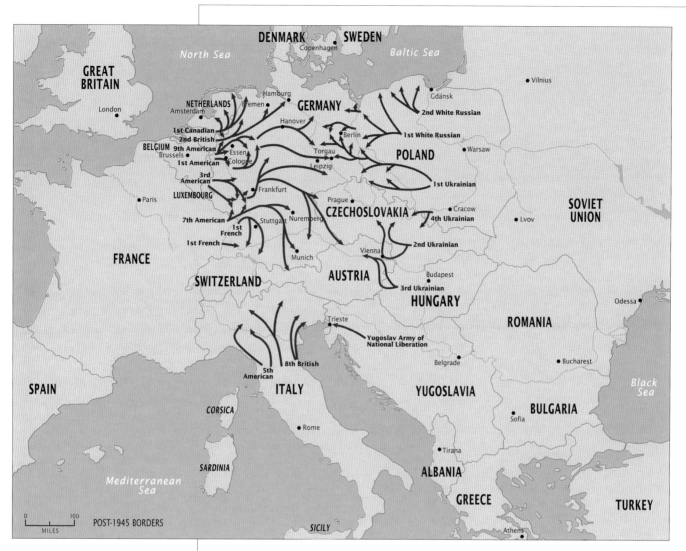

Allied Advances, 1945

Western Allied Armies ➡
Eastern Allied Fronts ➡

OPENING THE WESTERN CAMPS

In the war's final weeks, when the Americans and British entered Germany and Austria from the West in their final military advance, they came upon the concentration camps often by accident, usually meeting little resistance. Most of the troops, from generals to privates, witnessed scenes they could not contemplate as humanly possible.

As they entered the enclosed enclaves, the soldiers found dead bodies piled up by the hundreds along paths, roads, and train tracks. They encountered bent-over survivors, most in ragged striped prison uniforms; emaciated forms with body sores, bulging eyes, and maniacal looks. In sum, human beings who appeared less than human. Thus, describing the inmates he encountered at Gunskirchen, Delbert Cooper, an American GI with the 71st Infantry Division, wrote in a long letter home to his wife:

> I never want to see a sight again as we saw when we pulled in there. 1400 starving, diseased, stinking people. It was terrible. Most of them were Jews that Hitler had put away for safe keeping. Some of them had been in camps for as long as 8 years. So help me, I cannot see how they stood it. No longer were most of them people.

Former prisoners of the concentration camp at Wöbbelin, Germany, await transportation to hospitals for medical attention. May 4, 1945. (NARA)

They were nothing but things that were once human beings. . . . The people for the most part were dirty walking skeletons. Some were too weak to walk. They had had nothing to eat for so long. Some of them were still laying around dead where they had fallen. Others would fall as they tried to keep up with the truck. We were moving slow as we didn't want to run over anyone.

Recognizing his importance as an eyewitness to Nazi crimes, Cooper concluded his letter: "Please do me a favor and you or Dad type up this complete letter for me. Want to show it to people when I come home."[1]

Healthier prisoners in the liberated camps could walk or hobble, but thousands lay in wooden barracks in filthy and decrepit multi-tiered bunks. Most had been starved. Tens of thousands were sick. Battle-scarred soldiers and officers reacted physically to the results of the human depravity that the Germans and their collaborators had perpetrated on these slave laborers. The stench from the putrid odor emanating from both the dead and the living hit their senses first, the sights came next.

A myriad group of forced laborers had occupied these camps with names like Dachau, Bergen-Belsen, and Buchenwald. The Allies freed nearly 700,000 Europeans of various nationalities. The liberated included Jews and Gypsies who were usually quartered in the most deplorable sections of the camps, many Poles and other Slavs, prisoners of war (the majority from the Soviet Union, but some Americans as well), political prisoners, and homosexuals and others whom the Nazis considered socially aberrant. Of the 9 million Jews in German-occupied Europe, by May 1945 two out of three had been murdered; at most, 75,000 to 100,000 were alive inside the western camps at liberation.

"Doomed," *Chicago Daily Tribune,* April 21, 1945.

IN THE LIBERATED CAMPS

Upon liberation, prisoners were freed from the killing and terror inflicted by the Germans and their collaborators, but many still faced death from disease and malnutrition. The effects of prolonged starvation and brutal treatment continued to claim hundreds of lives each day. At Bergen-Belsen, which held mostly Jews,

13,000 internees died after liberation, often from mild cases of typhus that proved fatal to malnourished survivors. One physician with the Royal Medical Corps at Belsen, Lieutenant Colonel M. W. Conin, recalled how helpless he felt watching former prisoners die:

> Those who died of illness usually died in the huts, when starvation was the cause of death they died in the open for it is an odd characteristic of starvation that its victims seemed compelled to go on wandering until they fall down and die. Once they have fallen they die almost at once and it took a little time to get used to seeing men, women and children collapse as you walked by them and to restrain oneself from going to their assistance. One had to get used early to the idea that the individual just did not count. One knew that 500 a day were dying and that 500 a day were going to go on dying before anything we could do would have the slightest effect. It was, however, not easy, to watch a child choking to death from diphtheria when you knew a tracheotomy and nursing would save it.[2]

The first Allied medical units to reach the camps were attached to combat forces and equipped to give only the most basic care. More elaborate hospital units usually arrived within a few days of liberation, and organized evacuations of the sick began. Army doctors, nurses, medics, the Red Cross, and other relief workers struggled to feed and clothe tens of thousands of people and to treat and control typhus, tuberculosis, and other diseases that ravaged the camp populations. Medical teams dusted the survivors with the insecticide DDT to destroy typhus-carrying lice. They vaccinated the freed inmates and isolated those with contagious diseases. The squalid prisoner barracks were scrubbed, disinfected, or burned, often by German townspeople recruited for the task. Engineering units restored sewage, water, and electricity.

To help with spiritual needs, army chaplains conducted religious services, and thousands welcomed the opportunity once more to begin a life that had a semblance of normality. In addition to prayer, the survivors needed such basic staples as soap, toothbrushes, toothpaste, mirrors, hairbrushes, blankets, clothing, and sanitary supplies. The survivors required assistance to return to their former homes. They also needed help in finding relatives from whom they were separated during the war.

Gypsy barracks at Bergen-Belsen after liberation. April 17, 1945. (IWM)

Unfortunately, military units were not equipped to deal with all the physical and emotional rehabilitation that the survivors required. Extreme food shortages were the norm in devastated postwar Europe; adequate supplies and provisions were not available to the military units charged with assisting the camp populations. As a result, after the first few days of contact, food distributed to the survivors consisted of not much more than the bread, watery soup, and coffee that had been their diet under the Nazis. Nor was there sufficient clothing or sundries.

CONFRONTING ATROCITIES

On April 12, 1945, General Dwight D. Eisenhower, commander-in-chief of the Allied military forces, visited the Ohrdruf concentration camp. After viewing the evidence of atrocities, he ensured that these unbelievable scenes that "beggar[ed]

description" would be witnessed and documented so that firsthand testimony of the crimes could be given "if ever, in the future, there develop[ed] a tendency to charge . . . allegations [of what was seen at the camps] to 'propaganda.'"[3] Eisenhower ordered members of the U.S. military forces to see what had been done and urged politicians, dignitaries, reporters, photographers, and filmmakers to inspect the camps and describe the atrocities they saw to their constituencies. Subsequently, explicit photographs appeared in *Life* magazine, leading newspapers, tabloids, and exhibitions in the United States, Great Britain, and France.

Eisenhower and his subordinates also ordered nearby German townspeople to come and witness the results of Nazi depravity and to help clean up the areas and bury the dead. At burial services, Allied chaplains harshly reminded ordinary German citizens of their responsibility for the crimes. In Ludwigslust, Germany, for example, Army Chaplain George G. Wood said:

> Though you claim no knowledge of these acts you are still individually and collectively responsible for these atrocities, for they were committed by a government elected to office by yourselves in 1933 and continued in office by your indifference to organized brutality. It should be the firm resolve of the German people that never again should any leader or party bring them to such moral degradation as is exhibited here. . . .[4]

In a broad informational campaign in the occupied zones of Germany and Austria, the Allies distributed booklets with graphic photographs, such as *KZ*, a pictorial report from five concentration camps. The Allies also set up billboard displays and sponsored radio programs and film screenings. Almost everywhere, the Germans appeared to accept the facts of the atrocities but were reluctant to acknowledge responsibility for acts of their government. Most Germans were too busy focusing on rebuilding their lives, homes, and cities after the devastation of the war.

American soldiers view corpses at Buchenwald. April 30, 1945.
(AP/Wide World Photos, New York)

PURSUING THE KILLERS

Some former inmates wrought immediate, summary justice against their persecutors, and there was little the military could do to stop them. Both liberators and the liberated sought to punish those responsible for the atrocities in the concentration camps, and for the first few days after liberation, some ex-prisoners and Allied soldiers engaged in spontaneous acts of revenge. A number of SS guards, staff, and their collaborators were clubbed, stoned, knifed, shot, beaten, or otherwise molested. The freed prisoners wanted retribution; many Allied soldiers agreed that the guards deserved whatever spontaneous punishment they received.

The Allies had anticipated the need for punishing those responsible for war crimes, and formal procedures were pursued in apprehending and jailing individuals suspected of war crimes. In November 1945, the International Military Tribunal brought legal proceedings against the major Nazi war criminals. Conducted

The Dachau war crimes trial, December 1945. (NARA)

at Nuremberg, the former site of massive Nazi Party rallies, the trial lasted until September 1946.

In addition, smaller military tribunals run by Allied military authorities were conducted in the various occupied zones beginning in 1945. In three early military trials, justice was usually served: the director and key staff of the Hadamar sanatorium and the former commandants and a number of guards and other defendants from the Bergen-Belsen and Dachau concentration camps were convicted, sentenced to death, and hanged.

EUROPE'S DISPLACED MILLIONS

Well before the war in Europe ended, the Allies had made plans to assist millions of people uprooted by the war to return to their former homes. At war's end, an estimated 11 million people were classified as displaced persons (DPs), including former prisoners of war, forced laborers, and concentration camp survivors. The United Nations Relief and Rehabilitation Administration (UNRRA) had been established to work with DPs until relocation efforts could be completed. As temporary housing for the DPs, the western Allies used military bases, former prisoner-of-war camps, abandoned training areas, castles, barns, schoolhouses, and numerous other establishments. They also converted some concentration camps, including Bergen-Belsen and Dachau, into DP assembly centers.

Planners had not anticipated, however, that hundreds of thousands of people might not wish repatriation; nor did they consider the possibility that thousands would go back to their former homes and then return to Germany. Some Jews who had left the concentration camps or who came out of hiding returned to eastern Europe in search of loved ones. When they found no relatives, no restitution of their former property, and continuing antisemitism, most realized that they could not rebuild their lives in communities that no longer existed. Violent attacks against Jews in different parts of Poland also hastened the departure of Jews who had returned to their prewar homes. So they made their way back to Germany and into the American displaced persons camps, which had relatively lenient entry policies.

By September 30, 1945, the western Allies, assisted by UNRRA, had repatriated almost 6 million DPs. But nearly 1.5 million DPs still remained in Germany and Austria. Among them were about 32,000 Jewish and hundreds of Roma and Sinti (Gypsy) survivors. An estimated 842,000 Poles, many of them former forced laborers in the German war economy, made up the largest group of DPs unwilling or too ill to return home. Among the DPs were also many individuals who had collaborated with the Nazis and who feared retribution upon their return home.

Since supplies were limited, the DPs did not get everything they needed. UNRRA teams in 1945 were always understaffed and overworked; the military functioned well when it came to planning, order, and discipline but lacked the requisite skills of ministering to the emotional needs of people who had survived the conflagration. Moreover, the soldiers who had fought the war in Europe and liberated the camps were quickly demobilized or transferred to the Pacific theater for the war with Japan. Their replacements were young, inexperienced, and ignorant about the European wartime experience and the special needs of the DPs.

Perhaps the most egregious aspect of Allied policy was to treat DPs according to their nationality rather than their religion. The U.S. War Department revealed its rationale for not treating Jewish DPs as a separate classification in a handbook dated July 29, 1944, on "Military Government and Problems with Respect to the Jews in Germany":

Displaced persons prepare to relocate to another DP camp. Osnabruck, April 18, 1945. (IWM)

> As a general rule Military Government should avoid creating the impression that the Jews are to be singled out for special treatment, as such action will tend to perpetuate the distinctions of Nazi racial theory. In practice, Jews should receive the same treatment as other groups persecuted by the Nazis because of racial, religious, or political affiliation. Assistance should be based on need rather than preference.[5]

While in theory this policy may have been admirable, in practice it was incredibly cruel because Jews of Italian, German, Austrian, and Hungarian background were placed with others of their nationalities and categorized as "former enemies," while Balts (Lithuanians, Estonians, and Latvians), Poles, Ukrainians, and Yugoslavs, including those who voluntarily aided the Nazis, received special consideration as DPs because they came from liberated countries.

JEWISH DPS: LIBERATED BUT NOT FREE

By the middle of May 1945, word of cruel and inhumane treatment of Jewish DPs reached Washington. Jewish congressmen and community leaders contacted cabinet members who, in turn, appealed to President Harry S Truman. After some initial misgivings about the idea, Truman authorized an investigation of DP camps by Earl Harrison, former U.S. Commissioner of Immigration.

Harrison, accompanied by Joseph Schwartz of the American Jewish Joint Distribution Committee ("the Joint" or JDC), spent most of July surveying over thirty camps. His scathing report concluded:

> As matters now stand, we appear to be treating the Jews as the Nazis treated them except that we do not exterminate them. They are in concentration camps in large numbers under our military guard instead of S.S. troops. One is led to wonder whether the German people, seeing this, are not supposing that we are following or at least condoning Nazi policy.[6]

Harrison's report reached Truman's desk in August and had considerable effect. The president wrote to General Eisenhower about the Jewish DPs, ordering him to improve their accommodations, food, and clothing, separate them from former enemies and tormentors, and, in general, better the quality of their lives.

Eisenhower responded quickly to the president's directive. He deployed a Jewish adviser to help formulate military policy toward the Jewish DPs. He commanded subordinates to set up separate Jewish assembly centers, requisition German houses for DPs when necessary, and increase the caloric count of food rations from 2,000 per person to 2,500.

Eisenhower's orders were followed in some places but not in others. It was impossible to keep up with all the DP assembly centers since they frequently opened and closed. Hundreds, sometimes thousands, of DPs, Jewish as well as non-Jewish, entered on any given day; sometimes an equal number departed as well. Observers in 1945–46 counted from 300 to 500 DP centers of varying sizes.

At Eisenhower's directive, the army established 80 separate centers for Jewish DPs. While many centers showed marked improvement, some were still filthy, overcrowded, and rigidly organized; these conditions extended well into the fall. Eisenhower's Jewish adviser, Chaplain (Major) Judah P. Nadich, subsequently complained that many officers ignored Eisenhower's orders. On the other hand, as the general wrote to the president on September 18, 1945,

when it is realized that the Army in Germany has been faced with the most difficult types of redeployment problems; has had to preserve law and order; furnish a multitude of services for itself and the thousands of people it employs, and on top of this has had this question of displaced persons with unusual demands upon transportation, housing, fuel, food, medical care and security, you can well understand that there have been undeniable instances of inefficiency. Commanders of all grades are engaged in seeking these out and I am confident that if you could compare conditions now with what they were three months ago, you would realize that your Army had done an admirable and almost unbelievable job in this respect.[7]

Ignoring Harrison's recommendation that some Jews be admitted to the United States, Truman urged Great Britain to open the gates of Palestine to the Jewish DPs. The suggestion led to the establishment of an Anglo-American Committee of Inquiry that investigated whether Palestine could absorb more Jews. In April 1946, Great Britain rejected the Committee's recommendation that the Jewish DPs—whose numbers had grown to 100,000 by early 1946—be admitted to Palestine.

In the Jewish camps there were always shortages of material goods since the U.S. Army allocated a total of only 79 cents per day per DP for food, clothing, medical supplies, linen, and personal items. Black marketeers contributed to the economy by facilitating the exchange of goods. After the Harrison Report, voluntary social service agencies such as the Joint or the Hebrew Sheltering and Immigration Aid Society (HIAS) were allowed a much larger role and provided enormous help with sundries, letter writing, survivors' attempts to find lost relatives, the completion of necessary documents, and assistance in emigration. These Jewish agencies

Lt. Gen. Walter Bedell Smith, Chief of Staff of U.S. forces (holding bread slice), inspects living conditions in DP camp at Landsberg, Germany. December 6, 1945.
(Edward Clark, LIFE Magazine © Time, Inc.)

were godsends to the survivors, especially after the harsh and indifferent treatment they had been receiving.

Assembly center life in the fall of 1945, despite its difficulties and harshness, had some positive aspects. Individuals had a chance once again to order their own lives. Cultural and political affiliations were re-established and job training and educational programs became available. The residents of the camps also engaged in the normal activities of work, marriage, child rearing, re-establishing a semblance of community, and thinking about their future. If people wanted to live outside the centers, they could; but before leaving, the camps offered a time and place to consider choices.

To generalize more about the DP experiences in 1945 would be foolhardy. There were hundreds of thousands of Jewish and non-Jewish DPs and most of them had unique experiences. Some of the camps were good, others were not. The best that can be said for them is that they were a way station to another life for those who had been uprooted as a result of World War II.

No matter how harshly officers and soldiers sometimes treated DPs, it should always be remembered that the Allies had thought about repatriation of the displaced persons and had made plans to handle those ready to be rehabilitated. Unfortunately, the soldiers also had to deal with those who could not or would not return to their prewar homes, and these people presented problems that required political, not military, solutions. In retrospect, one must acknowledge that those in charge of the assembly centers tried to act in a responsible fashion. Unfortunately, they did not always succeed.

1. Yaffa Eliach Collection, Museum of Jewish Heritage, New York.
2. Paul Kemp, "The liberation of Bergen-Belsen concentration camp in April 1945: the testimony of those involved," *Imperial War Museum Review* 5 (1990): 32.
3. Alfred Chandler, ed., *The Papers of Dwight David Eisenhower: The War Years* (Baltimore, 1970), 4:2615–16.
4. Annex No. 4 to 82d Airborne Division After-Action Report, May 1945, RG 407, Records of the Adjutant General's Office, 82d Airborne Division, Box 11245, National Archives, Washington, D.C.
5. War Department, *Civil Affairs Guide. Military Government and Problems with Respect to the Jews in Germany.* War Department Pamphlet No. 31-121 (July 29, 1944), 4.
6. *Report of Earl G. Harrison: Mission to Europe to inquire into the condition and needs of those among the displaced persons in the liberated countries of Western Europe and in the SHAEF area of Germany, with particular reference to the Jewish refugees who may possibly be stateless or non-repatriable* (Washington, 1945), 9.
7. "Eisenhower to Truman," September 18, 1945, Eisenhower's Pre-Presidential Papers 1916–1952, box 116, file Truman-4, item 10, Dwight D. Eisenhower Library, Abilene, Kansas.

LEONARD DINNERSTEIN is Professor of American History at the University of Arizona, Tucson. He is author of *A History of American Antisemitism* (Oxford University Press, 1994), *Uneasy at Home: Antisemitism and the American Jewish Experience* (Columbia University Press, 1987), and *America and the Survivors of the Holocaust* (Columbia University Press, 1982).

THE LIBERATION OF THE CONCENTRATION CAMPS

Dachau, Germany, April 29, 1945.

(Bettmann Archive, New York)

Ohrdruf, Germany, after April 6, 1945.

(AP/Wide World Photos, New York)

Wöbbelin, Germany, May 6, 1945. (NARA)

Bergen-Belsen, Germany, April 17, 1945. (IWM)

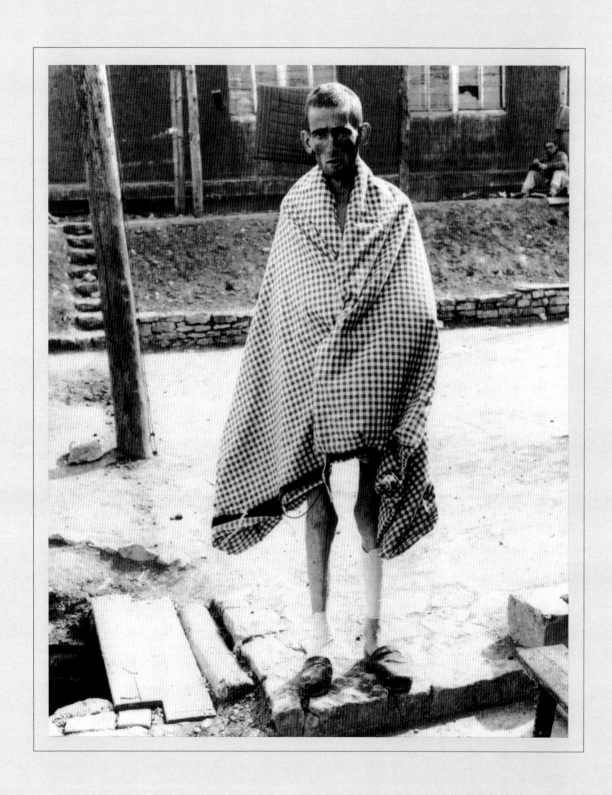

Buchenwald, Germany, after April 11, 1945.

(AP/Wide World Photos, New York)

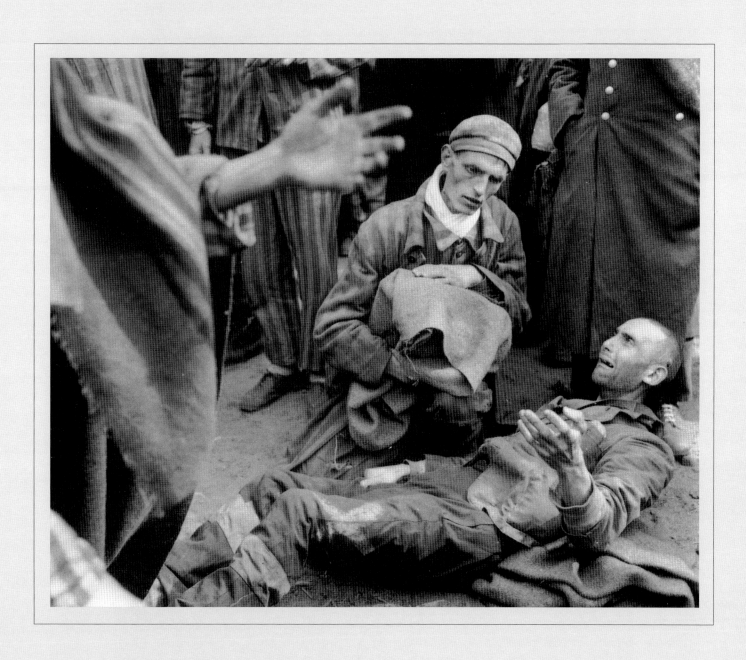

Wöbbelin, Germany, May 4, 1945. (NARA)

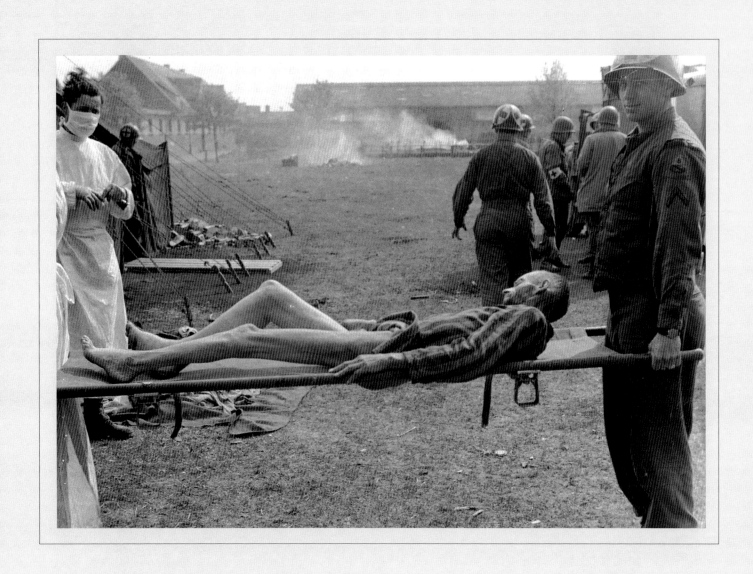

American medics carry a survivor to a delousing tent
prior to hospitalization. Langenstein, Germany, April 1945.
(Dr. Bernard E. Metrick and the 78th Medical Battalion Collection,
Photo Archive, USHMM)

A majority of concentration camp survivors were
men. At Bergen-Belsen, however, women far out-
numbered men. These women were photographed
11 days after liberation. April 26, 1945. (IWM)

Orderlies, wearing protective clothing against
typhus-bearing lice, evacuate a survivor to
a waiting ambulance. Bergen-Belsen, Germany,
April 22, 1945. (IWM)

Robert H. Abzug

Say the word liberation and images fill the mind. Crowds celebrating jubilantly, pretty women greeting proud and happy soldiers, champagne flowing like rivers through teeming public celebrations. Thus famous newsreels and photographs help shape the way we view the various liberations that progressively announced the end of World War II in Europe. But there are those other images, also labeled liberations and equally part of the story of World War II's end. They depict a dreadful repetition of faces without hope or comprehension, mounds of bodies piled neatly or littered about on the ground. These were the scenes that Allied photographers and soldiers recorded in the spring of 1945 at places called, among others, Dachau, Buchenwald, Nordhausen, Mauthausen, and Bergen-Belsen.

THE LIBERATIONS

These encounters occurred between the beginning of April 1945 through Victory-in-Europe Day on May 8. None involved major battles, nor were any of the liberations specifically planned. American and British troops happened upon these scenes of unexpected and unimaginable horror during regular military operations as Allied armies moved toward the eastern provinces of a fast-collapsing Nazi Germany.[1]

The first camp Americans liberated was Ohrdruf where, on April 4, 1945, members of the 4th Armored Division followed an escaped Polish prisoner into the compound. There they viewed prisoners' bodies strewn around the parade ground, bodies piled high in storage rooms, a vast funeral pyre, scores of half-burned and still smoldering bodies.

The GIs were so shocked by what they saw that their officers invited Generals Omar Bradley, George Patton, and Dwight Eisenhower to visit Ohrdruf to see for themselves. The visit occurred on April 12, the same day that President Franklin D.

Soldiers of the 42nd Division round up SS troops near Dachau. Late April 1945. (NARA)

Roosevelt died. Ohrdruf shocked even these battle-tempered veterans of two wars. "The smell of death overwhelmed us even before we passed through the stockade," wrote Bradley five years later. Patton was so upset that he became physically ill. Eisenhower seethed with anger. Soon after, he ordered every unit near Ohrdruf to visit it.[2]

Even as the generals toured this small subcamp, advancing Allied forces discovered greater horrors. On April 11, the 104th Infantry "Timberwolf" Division of the U.S. Army pulled into Nordhausen, in the Harz Mountains. Nordhausen supplied slave labor for the V-2 factories dug into surrounding mountains. The GIs discovered more than three thousand corpses and only fewer than a thousand enfeebled survivors.

On April 11 as well, members of the 6th and 4th Armored Divisions came upon Buchenwald in the beech forest above Weimar. One of the oldest camps (only Dachau predated Buchenwald), it housed thousands of prisoners living in vastly different conditions. Best treated were the German Communists, who effectively ran the day-to-day operations of the camps with the blessing of the Nazis. Worst off were thousands of Jews and Gypsies, wasting away in Buchenwald's *Kleines Lager,* or "Little Camp." It was from the "Little Camp" that the young Elie Wiesel saw the liberators.

Erwin Abadi, *Untitled,* ink on paper. Bergen-Belsen, 1945. A Hungarian Jew, Abadi was liberated at Bergen-Belsen. He created dozens of drawings and watercolors depicting life in the camp after the war, during his convalesence there.

(Gift of Eva and George Bozoki, Collections, USHMM)

Soon, discoveries of small and large camps and atrocity scenes became almost a daily occurrence. Perhaps the most awful was the British army's encounter with Bergen-Belsen. Once a small transfer camp, the population had swollen in the winter of 1944–45 to more than eighty thousand prisoners. Typhus began to spread and the Nazis cut off food and water supplies. Mass death and cannibalism resulted. One victim in March 1945 was the young Anne Frank. So bad were conditions at Belsen that more than 13,000 prisoners died *after liberation.* The British army needed bulldozers to fill mass graves with the dead. Such scenes, duly recorded for newsreels and magazines, engraved Bergen-Belsen in the minds of British audiences as a synonym for Nazi inhumanity.

For Americans, that synonym was Dachau, the first major camp of the Nazi system and in continuous operation since 1933. On April 29, 1945, units of the 45th and 42d Infantry Divisions entered Dachau. The 45th confronted a line of railroad cars piled with bodies, and wreaked revenge on remaining SS guards. Once inside the camp, they confronted an array of half-living, dead, or gravely weakened prisoners in the thousands.

Each discovery brought its own horrors. At Gardelegen, Americans found the charred remains of prisoners, sometimes frozen in their latest desperate pose of escape, in a warehouse set afire by the SS. Near Leipzig, another American unit found a similar scene. At Mauthausen and its subcamps of Gusen, Ebensee, and Gunskirchen, scenes reminiscent of Belsen greeted the liberators. At Mauthausen, Simon Wiesenthal fainted in the arms of his American rescuer. Landsberg, Wöbbelin, Flossenbürg, the list went on and on. Allied soldiers overran literally hundreds of camps and slave labor installations in Germany, the Netherlands, Austria, and France.

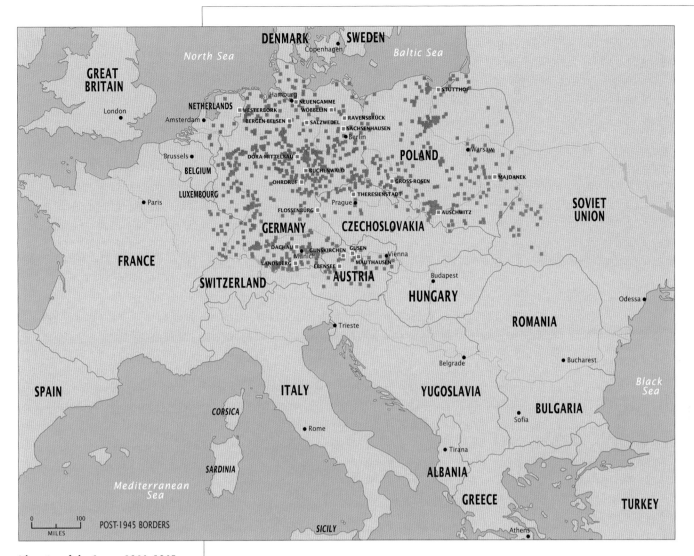

Liberation of the Camps, 1944–1945

Selected German Camps ▪

No wonder, then, the radio reports and official pronouncements that expressed total shock and dismay at these discoveries. No wonder that Dachau, Buchenwald, and Belsen were reported as "death mills" and "extermination camps," confirming every disbelieved wartime rumor and establishing the truth of Nazi genocide. At the time of these liberations, few doubted that the scenes discovered represented the worst of Nazi crimes, and that for Allied soldiers, governments, and citizens alike, these discoveries came without prior knowledge or warning.

We now know such characterizations were inaccurate. The liberations were shocking, but they did not reveal the first real evidence the Allies had of Nazi plans to destroy Europe's Jews. Nor were those camps liberated in the spring of 1945 the killing centers. They were not even the first to be liberated. The enduring significance of the Allied confrontation with horror in April–May 1945 must be viewed as part of a sobering historical reality.

We now know that the Allies began to receive word of the massive deportation of European Jews and their extermination at killing sites in occupied Poland—Auschwitz, Treblinka, Majdanek, Belzec, Chelmno, and Sobibor—soon after the killings commenced in 1942 and as the system developed through 1943 and 1944. Newspapers reported facts and scenes from reliable sources, eyewitnesses described what they had seen in the ghettos, at mass execution sites, and at

This pamphlet, issued by the 71st Infantry Division, typifies many publications by liberating military units. 1945. (Irving Heymont Papers, Archives, USHMM)

Army Talks, July 10, 1945. This issue featured a report on the atrocities discovered by U.S. troops in the liberated camps. (Kevin Mahoney Collection)

extermination camps. Allied intelligence units gathered accurate and detailed lists of camps and their functions.

Then, on July 23, 1944, the Red Army came upon the extermination camp of Majdanek as it advanced west across Poland. Here the Nazis had killed well over half a million human beings. The Soviets found only 700 gaunt but living prisoners; otherwise the camp was intact. Survivors showed them mass graves, gas chambers, and warehouses filled with eyeglasses, razors, children's toys, suitcases, and clothing. The Soviets invited select members of the Western press to tour the camp. "I have just seen the most terrible place on the face of the earth," wrote H. W. Lawrence of the *New York Times*. Several newspapers and magazines carried the story, but some wrote accompanying editorials that discounted the facts as Soviet exaggerations or fabrications.[3]

As the Red Army continued its offensive, it overran the already mostly sanitized sites of Belzec, Sobibor, and Treblinka. At these camps, the Nazis killed collectively more than two million persons, mostly Jews. Yet no survivors and few artifacts remained to tell the tale, and the Soviets issued no press releases on these camps. On January 27, 1945, the Red Army liberated Auschwitz, where they were greeted by fewer than two thousand Jewish survivors. An estimated 1.1 million persons, most of them Jews, had been killed at the camp. Although Auschwitz was by all accounts the largest of the killing centers, the Soviets hardly publicized its liberation at all.

Thus, the Soviet liberations of the extermination camps, those sites at the center of the Nazi system of genocide, hardly made a dent in Western consciousness. It was not simply that the Soviets made little of these events, and that few in the West trusted them. Both Majdanek and Auschwitz were liberated at moments when the military events of the war overshadowed all else. Nor did the cast of characters contain faces familiar to British and American audiences. Russian soldiers liberated anonymous, faceless victims of Nazism and showed off mostly the eerie but ultimately nonhuman evidence of the warehouses.

Yet in one crucial way, the Nazi abandonment of the eastern camps helped to create the shocking scenes discovered in the spring of 1945. Rather than attempting to murder those still alive in the camps, the Germans decided to march them through ice and snow or transport them on unheated trucks and trains, in the dead of winter, to camps in the west. Tens of thousands died on the way. Those who survived these "death marches" ended up in western camps such as Dachau, Buchenwald, Belsen, Mauthausen, and Landsberg. Most were in terrible physical and mental health and many were dying. Before this influx, these camps had been awful but *relatively* less murderous places of the concentration camp system. They were tough prisons mostly used to organize slave labor. Most of all at Mauthausen, many prisoners died of exhaustion, exposure, epidemics, executions, and starvation. Yet systematic mass extermination of prisoners by gas or other means was hardly known except on an experimental basis.

The influx of prisoners from the east swelled the numbers in these camps beyond the capacity of the Germans to keep prisoners even at a minimal level of

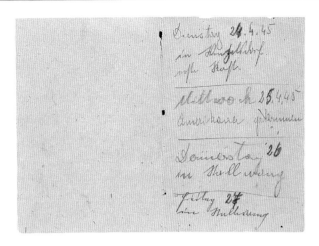

April 25, 1945, journal entry, "Americans have arrived," by Josef K., one of the thousands of homosexuals persecuted by the Nazi regime, liberated near Cham, Germany, while on a forced evacuation from Flossenbürg.
(Josef K./Wilhelm K. Papers, Archives, USHMM)

health. Epidemic disease, water and food shortages, and last-minute massacres and death marches created scenes far worse than confronted by any Russian liberator in 1944 and early 1945. The Nazi program of genocide, begun in secret and carried out systematically and scientifically in the hidden reaches of occupied Poland, now moved west for a final act of anarchic carnage, all before the unbelieving eyes of Allied troops.

American and British soldiers confronted scenes not only far worse than any discovered by liberating Russian soldiers at Majdanek and Auschwitz. They did so just as soldiers and the public had begun to let down their guard, expecting at any moment a bulletin that would announce the end of the war in Europe. Germany had been destroyed, its cities flattened by Allied bombing, its armies surrendering by the hundreds of thousands, its infrastructure collapsing. At this very vulnerable moment, the familiar, trustworthy hometown boys, the British Tommies and GI Joes, came upon not just warehouses and graves, but the vision of apocalypse—piles of bodies, human beings with but the smallest spark of life remaining, the broken, dying remnant of the Holocaust.

IN THE LIBERATED CAMPS

The tasks for soldiers, nurses, and civilians who entered the liberated camps were in many ways as unprecedented as the scenes they confronted. Simply surviving the assault on one's senses and sense of reality was a major challenge. Then came the vast effort to bury the dead, to restore basic services and supplies of food and water, and to save those who could be nursed back to life. Indeed, the reactions of Allied personnel to the camps and their actions to aid survivors in some ways constituted profound dramas in their own right.

To understand the soldiers' reactions, we must first understand that, by entering a camp, the American soldier entered another world. *Time* reporter Percy Knauth, after a few days stay, stated simply: "Buchenwald is beyond all comprehension. You just can't understand it, even when you've seen it." His exasperated exclamation suggested a truth about the camps: each constituted a universe unto itself, with a chaos of possibility and confusion and

"Freedom at Last from the 'Super Race!'" *Cleveland Plain Dealer,* April 11, 1945.

U.S. soldiers distributed K-ration packages in the camps after liberation.
(USHMM)

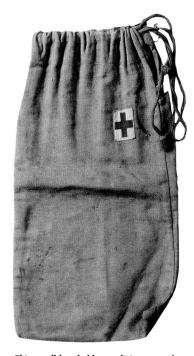

This small bag held a medic's personal effects. (USHMM)

awful reality that bore little relation to normal social and personal expectations and for which outsiders were never prepared. Comprehending that reality and describing it in language involves comparing it to, or fitting it into, an assumed human order and into the symbolism of language. Those who faced the camps strained at this task of comprehension precisely because a lack of perceived order compounded the horrors.[4]

Thus, for the liberators and war correspondents who entered the camps, not even experience with the battlefield dead and wounded quite readied them for the world inside the barbed wire. After all, in battle there are sides; there is a language for loss and gain; there is a logic to death, or at least a language of logic to ease the pain. In the camps, especially to the outsider, there was only chaos. Nothing made sense in this new world beyond the gates of Dachau, Belsen, Buchenwald, or Mauthausen.

The very geography of the camps often underscored this notion of two different worlds. "There are flower beds and trees," wrote an American doctor about the town of Dachau, "small shops, bicycles on the ground, churches with steeples, a mirror-like river. There was no intimation in this innocent-looking city of the activities a few minutes away." A visit to the sites of the camps today reveals that contrast. Buchenwald sits in a beautiful beech forest a few miles above the charming city of Weimar. Flossenbürg is but a short walk from the center of a quaint village and a peaceful, centuries-old ruin. GIs also noticed that, in quaint villages adjacent to the camps, citizens seemed quite hearty and healthy.[5]

The crossing of that line between the normal world and the universe of the camps caught even the most battle-seasoned veterans off guard and elicited reactions beyond words. At Dachau, American soldiers confronting a line of thirty-nine corpse-laden open freight cars vomited, wept openly, and crouched or paced in stunned silence. At Ohrdruf, General Patton became physically ill and retired

U.S. Army physician treats a survivor at Penig concentration camp, Germany. April 17, 1945. (NARA)

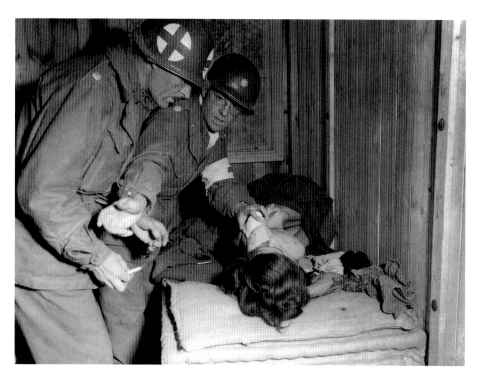

behind a barracks. At Buchenwald, a graves registration officer who had grown numb to the mangled corpses of his own buddies sobbed uncontrollably for minutes on end.

The intensity of those initial moments usually turned into what Robert J. Lifton has termed "psychic closing-off." GIs and other observers numbed their senses and emotionally distanced themselves from what was around them. Margaret Bourke-White, after photographing Buchenwald, wrote to her editor at *Life:* "The sights I have just seen are so unbelievable that I don't think I'll believe them myself until I've seen the photographs." In her autobiography she described a "protective veil . . . so tightly drawn" that she was emotionally blind to the scenes around her.[6]

This repression of emotion allowed soldiers and reporters to do their jobs, tasks that would have seemed ghoulish and perhaps impossible if thought about too much. GIs searched boxcars, barracks, and piles of corpses in search of the living. They supervised survivors or German prisoners and civilians in mass burial operations, or bulldozed the dead by the thousands into mammoth trenches. This emotional distance befitted the situation but stood out when set against the initial shock felt by new visitors. Thus in newsreels of Weimar citizens taking an obligatory tour of Buchenwald, one views shaken and tearful Germans leaving a barracks. In the background, an American soldier leans against a wall, blandly chewing gum.[7]

Such numbing was most effective in facing the mountains of dead. As for dealing with the living, the minds and emotions of liberators were strained to the limits. Revenge, of course, was the simplest option in confronting the Germans. Though most were treated as prisoners of war or handled through "proper" channels as potential war criminals, in more than the usual number of cases violations occurred. GIs at various camps gave their weapons to prisoners and watched them wreak revenge. Soldiers caught in the swirl of unbelievable carnage and combat-like situations sometimes participated. At Buchenwald, a group of American soldiers took turns pummeling recently captured guards. A squad of soldiers guarding more than a hundred captured Dachau guards lost control and machine-gunned them to death.

Much more complex was the stamp placed upon liberator visions of the Nazis' victims. On one level, the crucial level of action, most liberating American and British soldiers were sympathetic and caring. They shared food, ministered aid, helped make family connections—in short, did all the things they could to ameliorate an unbelievably tragic situation.

American soldiers speak to survivors at Buchenwald. April 18, 1945. (NARA)

At the same time, eyewitnesses often couched their descriptions of the dead and the survivors, either in memory or in contemporary description, in ways that distanced themselves from the victims. Often, the language of these descriptions dehumanized the dead and survivors. Malice does not seem to have been the main motivation or ingredient. Liberators desperately wanted to make some order out of the anarchy of death they saw, and in doing so, grasped at seemingly useful images. "After that first shock," wrote Curtis Mitchell, "you got over the feeling that these were people any more. They were so thin and so dried out that they might have been monkeys or plaster of Paris and you had to keep saying to yourself, these are human beings, and even when you said it your mind was not believing it. . . ." The most common descriptive word used to describe the stacks of dead was "cordwood," an ironic reference to German orderliness but also a testament to the need of eyewitnesses to create order out of chaos.[8]

As for the living—the survivors' gauntness, their nakedness, the drab and almost identical uniforms, and the language barrier that stood between most American and British soldiers and their new wards all contributed to a sameness that impoverished human understanding. One report made this point vividly: "Whether MICHELIN the tire magnate (now evacuated or dead), or ISAAC, the Rumanian Jew, a few months in the system made them indistinguishable, filthy, whining, clamoring bodies, covered with sores, which seem to be without souls."[9]

"Without souls." The phrase goes to the heart of a terrible irony. Given little in the way of normal human descriptive possibility, eyewitnesses often sought vivid images to express the horror of what they saw, images that, for all their power, reduced the humanity of the subjects. Take this description of prisoners in Buchenwald's infamous "Little Camp":

> On the sight of an American uniform a horde of gnomes and trolls seem to appear like magic, pouring out of doorways as if shot from a cannon. Some hop on crutches. Some hobble on stumps of feet. Some run with angular movements. Some glide like Oriental genies.[10]

At times survivors were compared to animals or as nothing. One reporter described two Poles as "whipped dogs" and "like dogs who expected to be kicked." "They were human skeletons who had lost all likeness to anything human," said

an observer at Belsen. A *Newsweek* reporter headed a section of his story about Nordhausen "These Were Men," and later described survivors as "creatures—you could not by any stretch of the imagination call them human beings. . . ."[11]

The case was different for some Jewish-American soldiers. Many were conscious that Jews made up a significant number of the victims in the concentration camp system. Some spoke Yiddish and therefore could communicate with the Jewish survivors. Others entered the camps with a sense of personal mission.

Morris Parloff, for example, an intelligence officer who came to Nordhausen several days after the liberation to investigate the V-2 factory tunnels at the camp, was eager to help Jewish survivors. This heady quest had already been sobered some weeks before when, in an occupied German city, he had come across a healthy Jew who offered to help Parloff in his work. The American thought it strange that there would be such a Jewish survivor in the city. Soon he found out that his helper had been a "finger man" for the Gestapo. For Parloff it was a shock to see what a per-

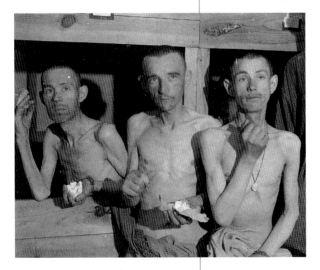

son might do to survive. He thought to himself: "How would I have done? Would I have had the courage to do otherwise?" "There was no way," he decided, "you could pass judgment."[12]

Nordhausen brought new and stranger experiences for Parloff. He got to the camp after most of the survivors had been taken to better quarters. He had expected to see an empty camp. Nothing had numbed his emotions, nothing had prepared him to repress the feelings that welled up when he found 120 Jews still in the tunnels. They had boarded the evacuation train like the rest, but were quickly thrown off by antisemitic fellow prisoners. Parloff welled up in anger at the Jews themselves for allowing this to happen. He felt shamed by them.

Later, while taking a tour of the camp conducted by a Jewish survivor, he had a more chilling experience. At one point, as Parloff stood in dazed silence before the crematorium, his guide climbed up and stood upon a pile of white ashes nearby.

"You know what I'm standing on?" he asked Parloff matter-of-factly, and then he began to tell him that he was perched on human ashes. "I screamed at him to get off," Parloff remembered, "and he looked at me very puzzled like what kind of morality is that? I realized I didn't understand him and he didn't understand me, and there was a great barrier between us. . . . I really felt alien, more than alien, it was through a wish that I wasn't fully aware of to dissociate myself: That is different . . . those people are different . . . I don't belong here."[13]

The raw contradictions that the GIs experienced were in a striking manner replicated by those who viewed the media accounts of the liberations. Two early reactions to the liberation photos boldly highlight this point.

In July 1945, the young Susan Sontag came across some photographs of Belsen and Dachau. "Nothing I have seen—in photographs or in real life—ever cut me as sharply, deeply, instantaneously," she remembered. "Indeed, it seems plausible to me to divide my life into two parts, before I saw those photographs (I was twelve) and after, though it was several years before I understood fully what they were about. . . . When I looked at those photographs, something broke. Some limit had been reached, and not only that of horror; I felt irrevocably grieved, wounded, but a part of my feelings started to tighten; something went dead; something is still crying."[14]

Alfred Kazin, who during the war wrote extensively about the fate of Europe's Jews, was stunned by the newsreels of the camps, in particular the films of Belsen. At a newsreel theater in London, he watched as

> sticks in black-and-white prison garb leaned on a wire, staring dreamily at the camera; other sticks shuffled about, or sat vaguely on the ground, next to an enormous pile of bodies, piled up like cordwood, from which protruded legs, arms, heads. A few guards were collected sullenly in a corner, and for a moment a British Army bulldozer was shown digging an enormous hole in the ground. Then the sticks would come back on the screen, hanging on the wire, looking at us.

"It was unbearable," Kazin recalled. "People coughed in embarrassment, and in embarrassment many laughed."[15]

In short, the confrontation with the camps hit the psyches of eyewitnesses and more distant observers with sometimes mutually exclusive demands: the demand to remember unforgettable scenes of cruelty, and the demand to forget the same scenes so that one could go on with one's life; the urge to render aid and sympathy to one's fellow human beings, and the simultaneous urge to distance oneself from the victims of horrors. Confronting the camps was unforgettable but unsustainable. One was changed by the event forever, but get too close, and one might be swallowed up in madness and death.

THE DAYS AFTER LIBERATION

For liberating soldiers and accompanying journalists, whose stay at a camp might last only a few hours or a day, the initial shock and numbing was often the final and lasting impression of the survivors and their world. Those who were called in to render long-term aid gained a longer, more complex, and ultimately more

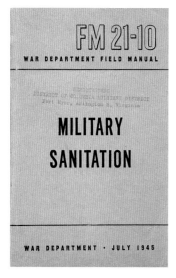

This military sanitation field manual spelled out basic guidelines for hygiene in liberated camps. (Kit Cooper Collection)

Flag used at liberated Terezin warned of the presence of typhus.

(Terezin Memorial, Terezin, Czech Republic)

Protective suit worn during treatment of typhus patients at Terezin.

(Terezin Memorial, Terezin, Czech Republic)

human vision of the situation. Many who came to the camps after liberation were granted the privilege of participating in the alleviation of suffering and the return to normal life for at least some of their patients. Yet doctors, nurses, and their support staffs faced tasks that seemed well-nigh impossible immediately after liberation. In the worst case of Belsen, doctors faced 25,000 survivors suffering from typhus, tuberculosis, malnutrition, and related ailments. At first, a thousand died each day despite the presence of the British and the beginnings of relief efforts. Similar conditions plagued American doctors at Gusen and Ebensee, while at Buchenwald and Dachau significant portions of the survivor population were in equally bad health.

The first task was to obtain enough food and water to begin to nurse survivors back to life. Liberators and those who relieved them secured these supplies from local towns, from army rations, and from relief shipments. The survivors themselves were so hungry that many ate anything they could find. One American doctor at Ebensee remembered putting down a box of soap, and returning a few minutes later to find that survivors had eaten half of it. The same doctor watched five men drop dead while waiting for their first real meal.

Simply honoring the dead became a challenge. Allied troops forced captured German guards and camp functionaries as well as local townspeople to bury the dead or rebury those previously placed in mass graves. At camps like Wöbbelin, where the numbers of dead were in the hundreds or low thousands, American and British personnel insisted on individual (if anonymous) grave markers for each victim. Sometimes victims were placed in neat, numbered rows. In the worst situations, where health concerns dictated quick and unceremonious burial, Allied soldiers had Germans dig and fill mass graves. At Belsen, the threat of typhus was so

Erwin Abadi, *Typhus*, watercolor and ink on paper. Bergen-Belsen, May 1945.

(Gift of Eva and George Bozoki, Collections, USHMM)

U.S. troops at entrance to Buchenwald concentration camp. Spring 1945. (NARA)

Crippled Polish and Russian prisoners at Mauthausen, Austria. May 6, 1945. (NARA)

great that the British used bulldozers to push bodies by the thousands into vast pits.

For the living and barely living, the Allies replaced the makeshift efforts of individual medics with field hospitals, sometimes several from different nations at a single camp, which in some cases had capacities for thousands of sick survivors. The relief administrators assigned as many as two or three doctors to each barracks, saving only the worst cases for the hospital. Yet quite often, even weeks after liberation, such major efforts failed to catch up to the destruction wrought by camp life. One medical report at Dachau, dated May 15 (two-and-a-half weeks after liberation), speaks volumes. Almost six thousand survivors were still hospitalized, more than the number of beds, and in both barracks and hospitals most still slept more than one to a cot. Sixty-seven died that one day, more than a hundred contracted typhus, hundreds more were transferred to the two hospitals, and foodstuffs, though increasing, were still insufficient. It was, according to another doctor at another camp, "a matter of constantly butting our heads against a wall."[16]

At first, these personnel often envisioned the survivors in the same manner as those who viewed them at the liberations—as vacant beings who had lost their humanity. Yet doctors and nurses and those attached to the hospitals had the distinct privilege of watching those who survived emerge as new persons. "Ulcers, static for weeks," wrote one British nurse, "began to grow in from the edges with healthy, pink granulations. Bronchitis and dysentery were brought under control. Hair thickened on shaven heads and stringy muscles toughened."[17] The spirit returned, grim but ready to face life again.

Yank, the Army Weekly, May 20, 1945.

(Gift of Anonymous Donor, Collections, USHMM)

As health reappeared and survivors clamored to leave the camps, new problems arose. Old national and racial prejudices broke out. Poles at Dachau, for instance, attempted to prevent the holding of Jewish religious services. Various national committees jockeyed for preferential treatment. Jews, not originally classified as a separate group despite their patently special status, fought to be considered apart from the national groups in which they were classified. In the end, within the year the vast majority of these liberated camp survivors had returned home.

Some groups could not or would not go home. Now called "displaced persons," they remained in camps (sometimes against their will) or lived within German society while waiting for an alternative. Many Jews, who felt no comfort in returning to Poland and other countries in eastern Europe, preferred to wait patiently for permission to emigrate to Palestine or to other countries in Europe or the Americas. Some Jews needed a longer period of recovery because of the extreme physical and mental punishment they had endured in the camps. Some Russians and Poles hoped to avoid returning to the Soviet Union or to the new Communist regime in Warsaw. Whether electing to stay in Germany for a while or to go home, what had been the shock and joy of liberation turned into the complicated process of recovering a life. Those "sticks" that had stared at Alfred Kazin in the darkness of a London theater, flesh refurbished but with minds tormented by the past, now struggled step-by-step to reenter the world from which they had been so summarily torn just a few long years before.

1. Unless otherwise noted, I have drawn the sources for this essay from the more detailed account in my book, *Inside the Vicious Heart: Americans and the Liberation of Nazi Concentration Camps* (New York, 1985).
2. Omar Bradley, *A Soldier's Story* (New York, 1951), 538–39.

3. H. W. Lawrence in the *New York Times*, August 30, 1944. One can track the general press reaction to news of various stages of the Holocaust in Deborah Lipstadt, *Beyond Belief: The American Press and the Coming of the Holocaust, 1933–45* (New York, 1986).

4. Percy Knauth, "Buchenwald," *Time*, April 30, 1945, 43.

5. Marcus J. Smith, *Dachau: The Harrowing of Hell* (Albuquerque, 1972), 79.

6. Robert J. Lifton, *Death in Life: Survivors of Hiroshima* (New York, 1967), 31–34 and passim.; Margaret Bourke-White, *Portrait of Myself* (New York, 1963), 259.

7. This scene can be viewed in *Nazi Concentration Camps,* a compilation of Signal Corps footage on various liberated camps available through the National Archives.

8. Narrative of Curtis Mitchell in "The Valley of Death, the Armies of Life," *Moment,* October 1981, 19.

9. Egon W. Fleck and Edward A. Tenenbaum, "Buchenwald: Preliminary Report," National Archives, Washington, D.C., SHAEF/G-5/2711/7.21, 13.

10. Ibid.

11. Frederick Graham, "300 Buried Alive by Retreating SS," *New York Times*, April 22, 1945; "Nazi Troops Bury Dead," *New York Times,* April 21, 1945; Gene Currivan, "Those Who Didn't Weep Were Ashamed," *New York Times*, April 18, 1945; Al Newman, "Nordhausen: A Hell Factory Worked By the Living Dead," *Newsweek,* April 23, 1945, 51.

12. Interview of Morris Parloff, Witness to the Holocaust Project, Emory University, Atlanta, Georgia.

13. Ibid.

14. Susan Sontag, *On Photography* (New York, 1977), 19–20.

15. Alfred Kazin, *Starting Out in the Thirties* (New York, 1965), 166.

16. William V. McDermott, "The Aftermath of Surrender," *Harvard Medical Alumni Bulletin* (Spring 1993).

17. Brenda McBryde, *A Nurse's War* (Essex, England, 1993), 170–71.

ROBERT H. ABZUG is Director of the American Studies Program in the Department of American Studies and History at the University of Texas, Austin. He is the author of *Inside the Vicious Heart: Americans and the Liberation of Nazi Concentration Camps* (Oxford University Press, 1985). Professor Abzug is currently preparing a documentary text on America's reaction to Nazi genocide during World War II.

CONFRONTING ATROCITIES

Captured SS guards at Bergen-Belsen load
corpses of victims onto trucks for transport to
mass graves. April 17, 1945. (IWM)

Germans forced to view one of the 800 murdered
prisoners whose bodies were found near Namering,
Germany. May 17, 1945. (NARA)

German civilians ordered to carry victims of SS
killings for proper burial in a cemetery. Neunburg,
Germany, April 29, 1945. (NARA)

American soldiers view corpses at Buchenwald.
April 11, 1945. (William A. Scott III)

U.S. congressmen inspect crematoria at Buchenwald.
Behind Sen. Alben W. Barkley (D-Ky) are Rep.
Edward V. Izac (D-Cal), Rep. John M. Vorys (R-Ohio),
Rep. Dewey Short (R-Mo), and Sen. C. Wayland Brooks
(R-Ill). April 24, 1945. (NARA)

Citizens of Linz, Austria, look at photographs of Nazi
atrocities. Such displays were mounted across American-
occupied Germany and Austria. 1945. (NARA)

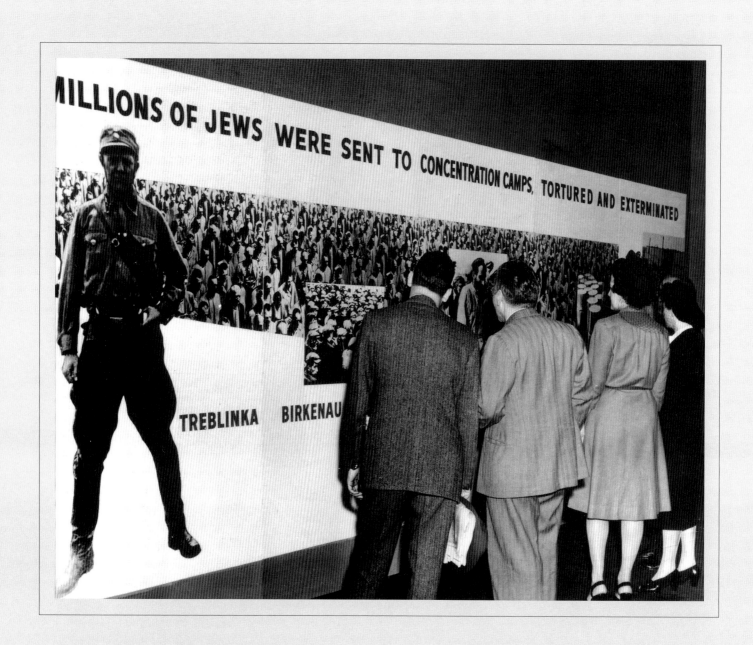

The Jewish Labor Committee organized the first
exhibition in the U.S. about the mass murder of European
Jews. New York, April 19, 1945.

(Robert F. Wagner Labor Archives, New York University, New York)

Sybil Milton

SS women guards load bodies for burial in a mass grave. Bergen-Belsen, April 1945.
(George Rodger, LIFE Magazine © Time, Inc.)

As World War II in Europe ended in May 1945 and British and American troops opened the western concentration camps, the Allied nations were suddenly confronted with the reality of Nazi criminality. Newspapers and newsreels everywhere carried photographs showing horrified Allied soldiers and dignitaries looking upon the dead and dying. Almost immediately, the western Allies began to collect documents, photographs, and eyewitness testimonies that would corroborate the horrors experienced and witnessed. The Allies also used this material in a publicity campaign to re-educate the public in occupied Germany and Austria as well as to inform the citizens of the United States and Great Britain.

Similar scenes of carnage had been previously described in the Anglo-American press after the opening of Majdanek by Soviet troops in late July 1944, although only a limited number of photographs of building exteriors, Zyklon B canisters, victims' identity cards, and piles of shoes were published in the *Illustrated London News* and in *Life* magazine. On October 14, 1944, the *Illustrated London News* noted apologetically that

An SS commandant, wearing civilian clothes, is forced to stand amid prisoners' corpses under the watch of an American guard. Landsberg, Germany, April–May 1945. (USHMM)

it is not the custom of "The Illustrated London News" to publish photographs of atrocities, but in view of the fact that the enormity of the crimes perpetrated by the Germans is so wicked that our readers, to whom such behaviour is unbelievable, may think the reports of such crimes exaggerated or due to propaganda, we consider it necessary to present them, by means of the accompanying photographs, with an irrefutable proof of the organized murder of between 600,000 and 1,000,000 helpless persons at Majdanek Camp near Lublin. And even these pictures are carefully selected from a number which are too horrible to reproduce. . . . The story is almost incredible in its bestiality. . . .

This explicit coverage met with incredulity in the United States and Great Britain because of skepticism resulting from knowledge of the exaggerations of World War I propaganda, the limited coverage of German killing centers in the Western press during the preceding war years, and the lack of direct confirmation of Soviet reports by the liberating armies in western Europe until nearly ten months later. The western Allies had entered deserted camps at Breendonck in Belgium in early September 1944 and at Natzweiler in eastern France in late November. Furthermore, several months later, in late January and early February 1945, the press paid scant attention to the liberation of Auschwitz.

Germans file past exhumed bodies. Volary, Czechoslovakia, May 11, 1945. (NARA)

It was thus only with the liberation of the western concentration camps in late April and early May 1945 that Anglo-American public realization of German atrocities overcame disbelief. The extensive photographic and press coverage after mid-April horrified the public at home and created empathy with the victims. These graphic images and eyewitness reports were believed because they were taken and transmitted by American correspondents and photographers under U.S. Army auspices.

Often the home public also received information in private letters from relatives serving in Europe. Thus, the Protestant U.S. Army Chaplain James B. Ficklen wrote to his wife from Ohrdruf:

I took pictures of this unbelievable scene to make it clear to people at home that the accounts of German oppression and murder in concentration camps . . . is all too true. I saw dozens of skeleton-like bodies. . . . I saw other things that will hardly do to write about. This was a hell on earth if there ever was one. This is the sort of oppression that is being ended by Allied victory in Europe. . . .[1]

The fact that the western camps had not been killing centers like Majdanek and Auschwitz did not matter, since the Anglo-American liberators witnessed the nightmare of overcrowded camps that had become death traps in the last months of the war. Moreover, the explicit photographic, film, and text coverage, which reached the home front after years of partial censorship and news blackouts, credibly conveyed to a wider Allied public the reality of mass death at the hands of the Nazis. A Mass Observation survey of British public opinion, for example, revealed the emotional impact of explicit media coverage. In mid-April 1945, 81 percent believed that "atrocity stories about the Germans were true," whereas in early December 1944, only 37 percent had accepted the accuracy of similar evidence.[2]

Wooden coffins were used to bury victims exhumed from shallow mass graves.
(Terezin Memorial, Terezin, Czech Republic)

MEDIA COVERAGE OF THE WESTERN LIBERATED CAMPS

In the spring of 1945, widespread media coverage followed Allied military commanders' inspection of the liberated camps and visits by reporters, U.S. congressmen, and other dignitaries. On April 12, 1945, General Dwight D. Eisenhower, together with Generals George Patton and Omar Bradley, inspected conditions at liberated Ohrdruf; on April 13, Eisenhower toured the just liberated Buchenwald concentration camp. On April 15, Eisenhower cabled General George C. Marshall:

> The things I saw beggar description. . . . The visual evidence and the verbal testimony of starvation, cruelty, and bestiality were so overpowering as to leave me a bit sick. In one room, where they were piled up twenty or thirty naked men, killed by starvation, George Patton would not even enter. He said he would get sick if he did so. I made the visit deliberately, in order to be in position to give *first-hand* evidence of these things if ever, in the future, there develops a tendency to charge these allegations merely to "propaganda."[3]

Lee Miller, then accredited to British *Vogue* magazine, was the only female combat photographer to follow the Allied advance across Europe. In her notes, hastily typed in a moving jeep and sent to Audrey Withers, her friend and confidante as well as her editor at *Vogue*, Miller described the scenes encountered when Buchenwald and Dachau were liberated. After seeing Buchenwald on April 12, Miller wrote: "Just read the daily press and believe every word of it. I would be very proud of Vogue if it would run a picture of some of the ghastliness." She also commented about the enforced educational excursions for American non-front-line units and local Germans citizens to look at the camp: "The tourists invited by General Patton fainted all over the place, although some remained arrogant. Even after the place was ninety-five percent cleaned up, soldiers who are used to battle casualties lying in ditches for weeks are sick and miserable at what they see here."

Survivors describe camp brutality to American soldiers. Buchenwald, April 26, 1945. (NARA)

Miller wrote Withers from Dachau that "soldiers were encouraged to 'sight see' around the place, they are abetted to photograph it and tell the folks back home. However, by midday, only the press and medics were allowed in the buildings, as so many really tough guys had become sick it was interfering with duties." *Vogue* was reluctant to print Lee Miller's "brutally frank" photos and they were only published belatedly in June 1945, under the title "Believe It!"[4]

On April 18, 1945, Eisenhower also sent photographs of the camps to Churchill, and on April 19, Eisenhower drafted a second cable to General Marshall:

> If you would see any advantage in asking about a dozen leaders of Congress and a dozen prominent editors to make a short visit to this theater in a couple of C-54's, I will arrange to have them conducted to one of these places where the evidence of bestiality and cruelty is so overpowering as to leave no doubt in their minds about the normal practices of the Germans in these camps. I am hopeful that some British individuals in similar categories will visit the northern area to witness similar evidence of atrocity.[5]

On April 19, Marshall informed Eisenhower that his suggestion had been approved by Secretary of War Henry L. Stimson and President Franklin D. Roosevelt.

Eisenhower had already sent Edward R. Murrow of CBS into Buchenwald on April 15 to do a live radio broadcast about conditions in the liberated camp; many British and American newspapers printed this classic account verbatim. On that same day, *Life* photographer Margaret Bourke-White described the "air of unreality" about her encounter with Buchenwald:

> I kept telling myself that I would believe that indescribably horrible sight in the courtyard before me only when I had a chance to look at my own photographs. Using the camera was almost a relief; it interposed a slight barrier between myself and the white horror in front of me. This whiteness had the fragile translucence of snow, and I wished that under the bright April sun which shone from a clean blue sky it would all simply melt away. I longed for it to disappear, because while it was there I was reminded that men actually had done this thing—men with arms and legs and eyes and hearts not so very unlike our own. And it made me ashamed to be a member of the human race.[6]

On April 18, an additional delegation of American radio commentators, including Lowell Thomas and Quincy Howe, also visited Buchenwald during their tour of the war fronts. Several days later, on April 23 and 24, American Dakota aircraft (DC-3s) flew reporters from Swiss and Swedish news agencies to survey Weimar and the liberated Buchenwald concentration camp.[7] These journalists were given the by-then standardized Buchenwald tour that showcased stacked corpses outside the crematoria, the Little Camp where Jews and Gypsies were housed, instruments of torture, tattooed human skin and shrunken heads, and interviews with designated survivors as well as spraying visitors with DDT to prevent typhus. Similar visits for British and American VIPs soon followed.

Churchill had promptly complied with Eisenhower's invitation and ten members of Parliament departed on April 20, inspecting Buchenwald the following morning. Their report stressed "the general squalor and odour of dissolution and

disease that still pervaded the entire place," and they found evidence of "a policy of steady starvation and inhuman brutality," although since liberation the camp had been partly cleaned up. The tour for British members of Parliament coincided with an inspection trip by Rep. Clare Booth Luce (R-Connecticut). Shortly thereafter, ten other members of Congress followed. Deeply shocked, these first congressional visitors certified that conditions at Buchenwald revealed "sordid barbarism at its worst."[8]

These visits set the tone for subsequent eyewitness accounts and photographs published by official delegations of American journalists, broadcasters, and members of Congress in the three weeks preceding V-E (Victory in Europe) day. A twelve-member bipartisan delegation from the House and Senate visited Buchenwald on April 24, Nordhausen on May 1, and Dachau on May 2. This group included Senator Alben W. Barkley (D-Ky), the Senate Democratic majority leader and later Truman's vice-president; Sen. Walter F. George (D-Ga), acting chairman of the Committee on Foreign Relations; Sen. Elbert D. Thomas (D-Utah), chairman of the Committee on Military Affairs; and Rep. R. Ewing Thomason (D-Tex), senior member of the House Military Affairs Committee. Senator Barkley presented their official report to Congress on May 15, indicting the "calculated and diabolic program of planned torture and extermination."[9]

In the last week of April and first week of May, eighteen American editors and publishers representing a cross-section of major American newspapers and magazines inspected both Buchenwald and Dachau. Among others, the delegation included executive editors from the *New York Times, Chicago Sun, Houston Chronicle, Los Angeles Times, New Orleans Times-Picayune, Minneapolis Star Journal, Kansas City Star, Collier's, Reader's Digest,* and directors of Hearst Publications and the Scripps Howard Newspaper Alliance. Joseph Pulitzer, editor of the *St. Louis Post-Dispatch,* explained: "I came here in a suspicious frame of mind, feeling that I would find many of the terrible reports that have been printed in the United States before

I left were exaggerations, and largely propaganda. . . . They have been understatements."[10] Similarly, Ben Hibbs, editor of the *Saturday Evening Post*, indicted Nazi brutality in his article "Journal to a Shattered World":

> Since my return to the United States, I have been asked by many people if the concentration camps were as bad as the newspapers have been saying. I can answer in one word: Worse. The war correspondents did a good job of factual reporting, but there is a limit to what can be said in words and pictures. You have to walk into one of those places and smell the unspeakable stench, not only of the dead but of the living. . . . You have to walk through the barracks, with their tier on tier of filthy, crowded bunks, and see the living skeletons dying of disease and starvation, too weak even to venture outside and enjoy their day of liberation. . . . Before you go into one of these pest holes, you are given typhus shots and doused with DDT powder to keep off crawling death. Yet when you come out you feel that you will never be clean again. . . . You know that as long as you live you'll never quite be able to get the stink of the place out of your nostrils, nor forget the scenes of abject misery you have seen.[11]

Among the last delegations to visit Buchenwald in the last week of April were representatives of twelve nations serving on the United Nations War Crimes Commission, several American labor leaders, and a group of American clergy.[12] Inevitably, Eisenhower became weary of continual interruptions caused by visiting dignitaries. Moreover, civilian visitors were discouraged from visiting liberated camps where conditions had substantially improved; they were also stopped from inspecting those camps that had been placed under quarantine because of actual or potential epidemics. Thus, on May 4, General Eisenhower cabled General Marshall requesting that VIP visits be discontinued: "My own belief is that if America is not now convinced, in view of the disinterested eyewitnesses we have already brought over, it would be almost hopeless to convince them through bringing anyone else."[13] On May 9, General Omar Bradley transmitted a "secret priority" message from the First Army to European theater headquarters, recommending an end to these incessant junkets:

> Buchenwald concentration camp has been cleaned up, the sick segregated and burials completed to such an extent that very little evidence of atrocities remain. This negatives [sic] any educational value of having various groups visit this camp to secure first hand information of German atrocities. In fact, many feel quite skeptical that previous conditions actually existed. Suggest that further visits to this camp be discontinued.[14]

Thereafter, only technical and medical teams and Allied personnel assembling evidence for the first trials visited the camps.

INFORMATION AND RE-EDUCATION IN OCCUPIED GERMANY

During the war, Allied civilian and military agencies made plans to educate German citizens about their individual and collective responsibility for war crimes. The Overseas Branch of the Office of War Information (OWI) developed a media strategy for Germany that mandated education about "German war guilt and German atrocities during the conduct of the war." In early December 1944, OWI issued long-range policy directives for re-education in Germany, "to create awareness of the moral issues involved in German aggressions. . . . Our primary task is to make *them* realize that they are guilty."[15] This policy, basically propaganda based on facts, encouraged photographs of SS concentration camp personnel and local German citizens being forced to assist in the burial of victims' corpses and compulsory tours of concentration camps under Allied armed military escort. It also involved extensive film, photographic, and newspaper coverage of Allied troops and military and civilian dignitaries inspecting conditions in the liberated camps. During the second half of April 1945, indelible images of instantaneous "retribution" abounded and the American press published photographs of German civilians and

Citizens of Schwerin, Germany, were ordered to attend funeral rites for victims. May 8, 1945. (NARA)

SS personnel forced to bury corpses in liberated concentration camps.

On April 16, a few days after liberation, Mayor Erich Kloss notified the residents of Weimar that they were required to visit the camp at nearby Buchenwald:

> The commanding general last night mandated that today at least 1,000 inhabitants of the city, half of them women, visit the Buchenwald camp and its infirmaries, in order to be convinced about conditions there, before they are changed. Individuals required to make this trip will include men and women ages 18 to 45, especially members of the dissolved Nazi party. Two-thirds are to be affluent and one-third should belong to the less well-off classes. They must be strong enough to endure the strain of the march and inspection (duration approximately six hours, about 25 km route). Provisions are to be brought, but must be consumed before viewing the camp. Nothing will happen to participants. The march will be accompanied by Red Cross vehicles and physicians to assist anyone who should be unable to cope with the exertions.

A one-page leaflet in German was also given to all visitors to Buchenwald admonishing them to:

> 1. Remember the whipping post, where people were beaten with cudgels!
> 2. Remember the crematorium ovens where tens of thousands were burned!
> 3. Remember the crematorium courtyard where piles of emaciated skeletons were stacked!
> 4. Remember the crematorium basement where innumerable antifascist fighters, including 34 British and Canadian pilots, were hanged!
> 5. Remember barrack 46, where human beings were treated like laboratory animals and infected with typhus bacteria!
> 6. Remember the stone quarry, where thousands were forced to carry the heaviest stones while running and being beaten, kicked, and shot!
> 7. Remember the Little Camp, where up to 2,000 individuals were crammed into special miserable quarters, including children ages 3 to 15!
> 8. Remember the stable, where 7,000 Soviet prisoners of war were executed by being shot at the base of the skull! . . .[16]

An identical flyer was printed in English for American troops stationed at the camp.

On April 17, Victor Bernstein, correspondent for the New York left-wing daily *PM*, reported from Nordhausen that "Yanks Forced Captured Foes to Smell the Stench of Death":

> [M]ilitary police of the 104th Division . . . rounded up civilians . . . to carry the bodies up on the hillside for burial in ditches by other German civilians. German families were ousted from homes in the town and several hundred survivors of the camp, strong enough to care for themselves, were moved in, with German women doing their cooking. This seems weak retribution for so heinous a crime. The question of the guilt of the townspeople for what happened at the SS camp is the same question in miniature of the guilt of the whole German people for what Hitler has done.

In a memorandum dated April 25, 1945, Lieutenant General Courtney Hodges of the U.S. 1st Army ordered German civilians to participate in the reburial of camp victims in the region under his command:

> Desire that as many of the civilian population as practicable attend the burials to be held unless obviously incapable. Cemeteries will be consecrated and will be con-

spicuously marked to serve as a constant reminder to the civilian population of the persons buried within. Roman Catholic, Protestant, and Jewish Chaplains will be used in each consecration and burial if available. If all three are not available for service at least one will be present. Where possible graves will be identified by decorous wooden cross or Star of David as appropriate.[17]

Allied commanders and information services also developed materials to re-educate the Germans, using photographic displays, publications, radio programs, and film screenings. Thus, on April 24, Charles Egan reported in the *New York Times:*

> Every German will view the pictures of inhumanities practiced on the prisoners at the Buchenwald, Belsen and other Nazi torture camps. Editorials from newspapers throughout the world showing the revulsion with which the Germans are viewed because of their treatment of prisoners will be "required reading" for all citizens of conquered Germany. Such a plan was being perfected tonight by information services of Britain and the United States in cooperation with Allied Supreme Headquarters. These services are assembling a pictorial layout of scenes at both Buchenwald and Belsen together with pictures of men and women wardens, who were captured at the camps. The photographs will be reproduced on large boards for display in every community in conquered Germany at points where inhabitants will be compelled to view them as they go to and from their homes. . . . Radio and motion picture programs bringing the same truths home to the conquered Germans will follow.

Moral certitude about using such previously inadmissible explicit images of corpses increased as the magnitude of similar Allied discoveries was corroborated in newsreel footage, photographs, and eyewitness evidence accumulated

Citizens of Burgsteinfurt, Germany, enter a movie house to view films of Nazi atrocities. June 1945. (IWM)

German POWs forced to watch U.S. Army films of Nazi atrocities. New York, June 27, 1945. (Bettmann Archive, New York)

The U.S. Office of War Information published and sold this pamphlet in Germany after liberation.
(Gift of John Peter, Collections, USHMM)

The U.S. 7th Army published *SS Dachau* after liberation and distributed it widely to U.S. soldiers.
(Martin Blumenson Collection)

from Bergen-Belsen, Ohrdruf, Buchenwald, Neunberg, Wöbbelin, and Gardelegen. The German committee of the OWI began collecting material for a two-reel film with the working title *KZ*, the German abbreviation for concentration camp, which it hoped to show at the founding conference of the United Nations in San Francisco. The London office of the OWI also prepared a pamphlet, *KZ: Bildbericht aus fünf Konzentrationslagern* [KZ: A Pictorial Report from Five Concentration Camps] to be sold for 50 Pfennig. The booklet provided a pictorial tour through atrocities in five concentration camps and was aimed at both German civilians and German prisoners of war. The Provost Marshal General's Office ordered more than 25,000 copies for distribution in German POW camps by or before mid-May 1945 and the Canadian government also requested several thousand copies.[18] This material was viewed with disinterest and indifference; although most Germans never doubted the accuracy of the photographs, they disassociated themselves from the perpetrators.

In June 1945, the British press covered German civilian attitudes in the town of Burgsteinfurt, known as "the village of hate . . . because of its silent resentment of British occupation." Two local teenage girls had "laughed at the horrors" during a mandatory film about Belsen and Buchenwald and were thus required to see the movie a second time. On May 18, ten days after V-E day, the first jointly produced Anglo-American newsreel, *Welt im Film* [The World in Film], was released for compulsory weekly viewing in the American and British zones of occupied Germany; a modified version was produced for Austria. Thirty-three newsreels were shown between May and December 1945; the fifth program on June 15, which lasted twenty minutes, was a German translation of an American newsreel showing scenes from thirteen concentration camps entitled *Atrocities Found in German Camps*. The thirtieth film released on December 11, 1945, focused on the opening of the Nuremberg trials. A majority of the *Welt im Film* newsreels emphasized German unconditional surrender, war guilt, the ruins of German cities, and trials and punishment for German war crimes. In mid-November 1945, the Americans tested a 22-minute version of the documentary film *Todesmühlen* [Death Mills] in Frankfurt; it was later released as noncompulsory without much publicity in January 1946.[19]

The Information Control Division of the (U.S.) Office of Military Government for Germany also published a pictorial magazine entitled *Heute: Eine Neue Illustrierte Zeitschrift für Deutschland* [Today: A New Illustrated Magazine for Germany]; the first issue was produced in London in June 1945 but only distributed in Germany in the fall. Modeled after *Time* and *Life* magazines, *Heute* was not intended "for entertainment." The magazine was to inform the German public about current political, social, and cultural events and to set an example of freedom of the press. Each issue emphasized the following themes: collective and individual war guilt of the Germans, the devastation and suffering caused by German aggression in other countries, the task of reconstruction and rehabilitation of devastated Europe, the role of the United Nations, and agreement with the principles and aims of the Allies. The main story in the first issue was about "People in the Hell of Concentration Camps" and its lasting impact on Germany's present and future. "The themes

"Wartime Portrait of a 'Good German,'" *Dallas Morning News,* May 6, 1945.

were no longer topical" because of the belated distribution of several thousand copies of this first issue. By 1947, *Heute* became "the channel for communicating to the German people information about the United States and the American point of view on world developments and on conditions and problems in Germany."[20]

Despite initial transportation and communications problems, the Allied information campaign reached a wide German public, although conditions were not propitious for acknowledging individual or colective responsibility for Nazi crimes. Most Germans focused on rebuilding their lives, overwhelmed by the problems of the physical reconstruction of ruined cities, food shortages, and the flood of refugees and expellees from eastern Europe. In June 1945, Morris Janowitz, an intelligence officer assigned to the Psychological Warfare Branch of the U.S. Army, analyzed the results of the first month of the education campaign in the American and British occupation zones:

> Within four weeks after V-E Day, almost every German had direct and repeated contact with our campaign to present the facts. . . . It appeared that British Broadcasting Corporation and Radio Luxembourg had been the main sources, although Allied-published newspapers were widely mentioned. Allied posters were less frequently specified. Almost everywhere one encountered acceptance of the facts, although frequently in an automatic fashion which bespoke a genuine lack of concern. . . .[21]

By the end of 1945, a limited number of licenses for German newspapers and books had been issued, and political re-education and denazification were being implemented in the American zone of occupied Germany.

INFORMING THE ALLIED PUBLIC ABOUT NAZI ATROCITIES

A parallel campaign to inform the American and British public about Nazi atrocities was more effective. The April 26th Paris edition of *Stars and Stripes* published a photograph of two children's corpses at Nordhausen. An accompanying editorial, "Cameras Spread the Truth," commented:

> The men who are fighting their way through Germany and laying open the stark, naked, rotten truth of the Nazi horror camps will be reassured to know that the world press is publishing the photographic evidence with unprecedented candor. Few of the pictures are for feeble stomachs. Few are of the type that any considerate editor would publish in normal times in a newspaper of general circulation. But in the belief that the public must know and must see to believe, even conservative publications are opening their pages to unretouched photographs of Belsen, Ohrdruf and Buchenwald. The displays are revolting and distasteful but they are bringing home to a civilized world as no other medium could the cold truth of German cruelty and sadism. . . . This is no carnival of horror inspired by a morbid thrill at seeing someone else's suffering. The reaction has been one of honest disgust and cold fury. . . .

On April 24, Harry Warner of Warner Brothers Pictures called Col. Frank McCarthy at the Office of the Army Chief of Staff in Washington, asking that "the film industry . . . be asked to publicize the atrocities through newsreels. He explained that every newsreel had a tremendous amount of footage on the subject, but that it had been withheld because the companies were afraid of making people sick in theaters and thus creating bad will for the theaters and newsreel companies. He felt that an appeal from General Marshall would smoke this footage out and into public view."[22] These newsreels were released throughout the United States by early May 1945.

Despite the educational importance of such newsreels, public opposition was anticipated. American audiences in that era, far more naive than today, "gasped with shock and revulsion" or viewed the footage in "stony silence." The manager of the Dallas Palace "got sick . . . seeing the films for the first time." Only Radio City Music Hall in New York refused to show these newsreels, since they "did not want to chance sickening any squeamish persons." Both the *New York Times* and *New York Herald Tribune* reported that British "moviegoers, unable to stomach atrocity newsreels, tried to leave a Leicester Square theatre but were turned back by British and Allied soldiers who told them to return and see what other people had endured. . . ."[23]

In early May, a second film opened to a mixed response in London at Gaumont "State" cinema on Kilburn High Road, where the theater marquee stated "Scenes of Unbelievable Nazi Atrocities at Buchenwald and Belsen; See Them—Lest You Forget." The cynical British audience interviewed after the film was indifferent and "fed up with pictures of dead bodies heaped on top of each other." Some expressed anger at the British government "which must have known all about it," and a few viewers "thought that the Allied bombing of Germany caused disorganization . . . making it impossible to run or supply the camps."[24]

A crowd lines up to see the *Daily Express* exhibition "The Horror Camps." London, May 1945.
(Hulton Deutsch Collection, London, United Kingdom)

A public opinion poll taken in early May 1945 revealed that psychological discomfort often curtailed the American desire to know the truth about Nazi genocide: 89 percent of the respondents felt that these "pictures should be shown to all German people in Germany," whereas only 60 percent thought it a good idea to have "movie theaters throughout the country [the United States] show these pictures." In the same poll, 39 percent wanted "to see" the films themselves, and 35 percent thought it "a bad idea" to show such films.[25]

"Horror Camps" exhibition at the *Daily Express* reading room. London, May 1945.

(Hulton Deutsch Collection, London, United Kingdom)

The traditional restraints of the 1934 Production Code forbidding explicit violence, cruelty, profanity, and "repellent subjects" by the Motion Picture Producers and Distributors of America (MPPDA)—popularly known as the Hays Office for Will H. Hays, Postmaster General during the Harding administration and later first president of MPPDA—had conditioned many Americans to avoid newsreels with Nazi brutalities. In late May 1945, the Hays Office withheld approval for a documentary film about the Kharkov trial based on Soviet and German footage. This film, entitled *We Accuse,* was deemed offensive because narration included the word "damn" and because the film contained "numerous pictures of bodies, skeletons, maimed children, and other results of German bestiality." Additional objections were registered about "the prolonged hanging" of four war criminals after trial. The feature-length documentary opened at the Little Carnegie Playhouse in New York but could not be generally distributed.[26] Nevertheless, by July, home-front audiences of invited journalists, teachers, and local Rotary Clubs in Dallas and other cities could see two U.S. Army films: *German Atrocities Unexpurgated* and *Your Job in Germany.*[27]

On June 30, 1945, the Library of Congress opened a photomural exhibition called "Lest We Forget," sponsored by the *St. Louis Post-Dispatch* and the *Washington Evening Star.* Both newspapers had participated in Eisenhower's Buchenwald and Dachau inspection trips. The *St. Louis Post-Dispatch* reported daily crowds of more than 5,000 visitors, despite a summer heat wave and a non-air-conditioned building. Attendance records revealed that 88,891 visitors saw the exhibition in three weeks. The Army Signal Corps provided films of German atrocities for screenings at the Library of Congress and for circulation to local high schools and community centers; crowds often necessitated additional showings.[28] This exhibition subsequently traveled to Boston, Cleveland, and twenty towns in Illinois and Missouri.

An earlier exhibition organized by the Jewish Labor Committee opened at Vanderbilt Gallery in New York from mid-April to late May 1945. Entitled "Heroes and Martyrs of the Ghettos," it stressed events in the Warsaw ghetto and occupied Poland. The exhibition had numerous prestigious co-sponsors, including union leaders; university presidents; the French, Czech, and Polish ambassadors to the United Nations; and celebrities such as Albert Einstein, Eleanor Roosevelt, Under Secretary of State Sumner Welles, UNRRA Director and former New York Governor Herbert Lehmann, and New York Mayor Fiorello LaGuardia. Another exhibition, called "Hitler's Crimes," opened at the Grand Palais in Paris on June 4, 1945. This exhibit was accompanied by an open-air mass and prayer service for deportees and prisoners; 100,000 people participated in the mass. In London, on May 1, the *Daily Express* opened a well-visited exhibition "The Horror Camps: Atrocities Revealed" in their Regent Square reading room and also at Trafalgar Square.[29]

CONCLUSION

By the end of 1945, the Anglo-American occupation authorities had distributed publications, exhibitions, films, and radio programs that told the full story of the Nazi concentration camps and the Nuremberg trial. Nevertheless, re-education, democratization, and denazification were initially only partly successful since the immediate postwar period was not propitious for reflections about the recent German past. Overshadowed by the problems of reconstruction and the Cold War, most Germans sought to build new lives denying complicity in Nazi crimes. Similarly, initial shock about Nazi atrocities in the United States and other Allied countries gave way to indifference. Repetition of films and photographs of German atrocities rapidly produced audience saturation and impatience with government "atrocity propaganda." Time had to pass before the Holocaust could be absorbed and understood.

The author would like to thank Steven Luckert, Carolyn Van Newkirk, Nicole Renvert, and Jürgen Zieher for their research assistance; John Taylor, Manchester, U.K.; and Cheryl Regan, Library of Congress, Washington, D.C.

1. United States Holocaust Memorial Museum, Washington, D.C., Collection 1986.031.24: letter dated April 15, 1945.
2. University of Sussex, Brighton, U.K., The Tom Harrisson Mass-Observation Archive, file report 2228: "Special Pre-Peace News Questionnaire," April 18, 1945, 14–22; photocopies courtesy of Professor John Taylor, Manchester, U.K. For an analysis of British public opinion in spring 1945, see John Taylor, *War Photography: Realism in the British Press* (London and New York, 1991), 62–66.
3. Albert Chandler, ed., *The Papers of Dwight David Eisenhower: The War Years* (Baltimore, 1970), 4:2615–16.
4. Copyright Lee Miller Archive, courtesy Anthony Penrose and Suzanna Penrose, Chuddingly, East Sussex, U.K., file 51, Buchenwald; file 54, Buchenwald and Weimar, April 12, 1945; Anthony Penrose, ed., *Lee Miller's War: Photographer and Correspondent with the Allies in Europe, 1944–1945* (Boston, Toronto, and London, 1992), 165, 187.
5. Chandler, *The Papers of Dwight David Eisenhower*, 4:2623.
6. Jonathan Silverman, ed., *The Taste of War: Margaret Bourke-White* (London, 1985), 261.
7. "Der Augenschein der neutralen Journalisten in Buchenwald," *Neue Zürcher Zeitung*, April 27, 1945 (morning edition).
8. *Buchenwald Camp: The Report of a Parliamentary Delegation* (London, 1945), 4, 7. For Clare Booth Luce, see "Mrs. Luce Visits Buchenwald," *New York Herald Tribune*, April 22, 1945; Library of Congress, Manuscript Division, (hereafter cited as LC), Clare Booth Luce Papers, box 678, folders 8–9: Address to House of Representatives, May 3, 1945. For comments by congressmen, see *Chicago Daily Tribune*, April 23, 1945.

9. 79th Congress, 1st Session, Senate Document No. 47, *Atrocities and Other Conditions in Concentration Camps in Germany* (Washington, D.C., 1945).

10. LC, Joseph Pulitzer papers, containers 97–98, reels 79–80; and William I. Nichols papers, files 19–25; Joseph Pulitzer, *A Report to the American People* (St. Louis, 1945), 94; and "Reflections on Atrocities," *The Bulletin of the American Society of Newspaper Editors* (May 1945), in: Pulitzer papers, reel 80.

11. *The Saturday Evening Post*, June 9, 1945, 20–22, 83–86; quotation on 22.

12. National Archives and Records Administration (hereafter cited as NARA), Washington, D.C., RG 331, Records of Allied Operational and Occupation Headquarters, World War II, SHAEF, G-5, 1711/8929/263, for visit by clergy and labor leaders; RG 338, box 444, United Nations War Crimes Commission, "Visit of Delegation to Buchenwald Concentration Camp in Germany," April 26–27, 1945.

13. Chandler, *The Papers of Dwight David Eisenhower*, 4:2679.

14. NARA, Washington, D.C., RG 331, Records of Allied Operational and Occupation Headquarters, World War II, box 50, SHAEF, G-5/2711/721: Telegram Twelfth Army Group, signed Bradley, to ETOUSA, May 9, 1945.

15. NARA, RG 208, Records of the New York Office, Bureau of Overseas Publications, entry 479, container 808: directive by Wallace Carroll, OWI Deputy Director, Overseas Operations, December 5, 1944, 7; emphasis in original.

16. Walter Bartel, Klaus Trostorff, et al., eds., *Buchenwald, Mahnung und Verpflichtung: Dokumente und Berichte*, 4th rev. exp. ed. (Berlin, 1983), 640–41.

17. NARA, Suitland, MD, RG 338, Records of U.S. Army Commanders, 1942–, box 1, HQ 1st Army file: 000.5, April 25, 1945.

18. NARA, Suitland, MD, RG 332, Records of U.S. Theaters of War, World War II, box 31, file 155: "German Prisoner Reactions to KZ booklet on Atrocities," Report no. 131, Surveys Section, Office of War Information, June 23, 1945.

19. *Illustrated London News*, June 16, 1945; Goethe Institut, ed., *German Newsreels 1933–1947* (Munich, 1984), 38–45; Brewster Chamberlin, "Todesmühlen: Ein früher Versuch zur Massen-'Umerziehung' im besetzten Deutschland 1945–1946," *Vierteljahrshefte für Zeitgeschichte* 29 (1981), 420 ff.

20. "Menschen in der Hölle der Konzentrationslager," *Heute* 1 (June 1945), 23–27; "The Development of Heute Policy," June 15, 1947, in NARA, RG 208, Records of the New York Office, Bureau of Overseas Publications, box 5, Office of War Information Overseas Publications; and RG 260, Records of the United States Occupation Headquarters World War II, box 247, Information Control Division.

21. Morris Janowitz, "German Reactions to Nazi Atrocities," *American Journal of Sociology* 52 (September 1946), 141–45.

22. NARA, RG 165, Records of the War Department, General and Special Staff, entry 13, box 133, Army Chief of Staff file 062.2, case 46: memorandum of telephone call from Harry Warner to Col. Frank McCarthy, April 24, 1945.

23. "Audiences Say Atrocity Films Most Shocking Ever Seen," *Motion Picture Daily* 57 (May 4, 1945), 1, 7; "Nazi Atrocity Films Real Shockers But US Audiences Take It; Some Cuts," *Variety*, May 9, 1945; "Horror Pictures," *Motion Picture Herald* 159 (May 5, 1945), 2; "Troops Make Britons See Newsreels of Atrocities," *New York Times*, April 21, 1945.

24. University of Sussex, The Tom Harrisson Mass-Observation Archive, file report 2248: "German Atrocities," May 5, 1945, 1–3.

25. Hadley Cantril, *Public Opinion* (Princeton, 1951), 489, nos. 49, 51.

26. Thomas Doherty, *Projections of War: Hollywood, American Culture, and World War II* (New York, 1993), 36–59, 244–50; *PM*, May 31, 1945; and John T. McManus, "The Guilty Die at Kharkov," *PM*, June 4, 1945.

27. State Historical Society of Wisconsin, Madison, Walker Stone Papers: Correspondence

between Rex Stout, Chairman of the Writers' War Board, New York, and Walker Stone, Scripps-Howard Alliance (NY) and Ted Dealey, *Dallas Morning News*, June–July 1945.

28. Martin Luther King Memorial Library, Washington, D.C., Washingtonia Department, subject file Library of Congress Exhibits, 1900–1946; "Atrocity Pictures seen by 10,814 at Capital in 2 Days," *St. Louis Post-Dispatch*, July 2, 1945; *Washington Star,* July 23, 1945.

29. Robert Wagner Labor Archives, New York University, Papers of the Jewish Labor Committee: Jewish Labor Committee, ed., "Martyrs and Heroes of the Ghettos: an exhibition dedicated to the Second Anniversary of the Warsaw Ghetto Uprising," New York, Vanderbilt Gallery, April 19–May 25, 1945; American Jewish Joint Distribution Committee Archives, New York: photographs of the exhibition from the French Press and Information Service, New York; Hulton-Deutsch, London, Daily Express photo archive; and University of Sussex, The Tom Harrisson Mass-Observation Archive, file report 2248: "German Atrocities," May 5, 1945, 3–8.

SYBIL MILTON is Senior Historian at the U.S. Holocaust Memorial Museum's Research Institute. She is author of *In Fitting Memory: The Art and Politics of Holocaust Memorials* (Wayne State University Press, 1991), co-author of *Art of the Holocaust* (with Janet Blatter, Rutledge Press, 1981) and co-editor of the 26-volume series, *Archives of the Holocaust* (with Henry Friedlander, Garland Press, 1989–95). She is currently preparing a book on photography of the Holocaust as historical evidence.

EARLY WAR CRIMES TRIALS

At Dachau, liberated prisoners confront an SS guard.
Behind them lie the corpses of SS guards shot by American
troops. April 29, 1945. (NARA)

British soldiers arrest a member of the SS. Germany, 1945.

(Bettmann Archive, New York)

An American army officer questions a former SS
guard accused of beating prisoners with the whip.
Lahde, Germany, May 4, 1945. (NARA)

SS guards at Bergen-Belsen, including the notorious Irma
Grese (#9), stand trial for war crimes. Lüneburg, Germany, 1945.
(AP/Wide World Photos, New York)

At the "Hadamar trial," the former chief nurse and
the head of the sanatorium confer with their German
counsel. Wiesbaden, Germany, October 9, 1945.
(Bettmann Archive, New York)

The Dachau military trial. December 4, 1945. (NARA)

Guards keep close watch over prisoners at the
Nuremberg jail. November 24, 1945. (NARA)

The chart identifies the positions IMT defendants held in
the Nazi hierarchy. November 22, 1945. (NARA)

James J. Weingartner

"Witnesses for the Prosecution,"
St. Louis Post-Dispatch, **April 30, 1945.**

A survivor gives evidence to Allied war crimes investigators. Vaihingen, Germany, May 1945.
(Main Crimes Commission, Warsaw, Poland)

In response to the unprecedented crimes committed by Nazi Germany during World War II, the major Allied powers adopted an unprecedented program designed to bring the criminals to justice and to prevent repetitions of Nazi criminality. The program evolved slowly and hesitantly, reflecting uncertainty as to appropriate procedures. Although quick to condemn German atrocities, including the mass murder of European Jews, British and American leaders were initially reluctant to engage in detailed preparation for punishing the criminals due to their preoccupation with fighting the war and fear of German retaliation against Allied prisoners. Not until October 20, 1943, was a United Nations War Crimes Commission established in London, followed in November by the Moscow Declaration in which Britain, the United States, and the Soviet Union, speaking for all 32 countries then at war with Germany, expressed their resolve to pursue Nazi war criminals "to the uttermost ends of the earth" in order that justice might be done. The declaration recognized two categories of offenders. Those whose crimes had been committed in a specific location were, at the end of the war, to be returned to "the scene of their crimes and judged on the spot by the peoples whom they have outraged." Others, "major" criminals whose crimes had no specific location, were to be dealt with "by the joint decision" of the Allied governments.[1]

Yet beyond a vague reference to punishment "according to the laws" of countries liberated from German control, which seemed implicitly to exclude "major" war criminals, the Moscow Declaration gave no indication of the procedure to be

used in accomplishing justice. At the end of 1943, the Soviet Union conducted the first war crimes trials of World War II, prosecuting and publicly hanging a number of captured Germans and their Soviet accomplices for mass murders committed in Kiev and Kharkov. But it was by no means certain that a precedent of conducting formal trials had been established. Much simpler methods of meting out justice had considerable appeal in light of the magnitude of Nazi crimes. Writing to his foreign secretary, Anthony Eden, in July 1944, British Prime Minister Winston Churchill expressed the opinion that Germans responsible for "butcheries" should be summarily shot after falling into Allied hands. U.S. Secretary of the Treasury Henry Morgenthau, Jr., also favored that approach, at least in regard to major Nazi leaders. Such attitudes had been encouraged by the Soviet army's liberation of the labor/extermination camp complex at Majdanek near Lublin, Poland, where evidence of the murders of hundreds of thousands of Jews, Poles, and others was made available to the Allied press. Limited summary execution came close to adoption as official Allied policy when, at the Quebec conference of September 1944, Churchill and Roosevelt agreed to recommend to Stalin that the three major powers compile a list of Nazi leaders to be killed upon capture.

An American soldier examines silverware plundered from prisoners at Buchenwald. May 5, 1945. (NARA)

Enthusiasm for the plan was far from unanimous. U.S. Secretary of War Henry Stimson urged that captured German leaders be given some opportunity to defend themselves by informing the prisoners of the charges against them and allowing them to respond and call defense witnesses. Not only would such an approach be more in tune with "civilized" conduct but, by producing a record of Nazi criminality for posterity, would make its recurrence less likely. In the face of press criticism of the "Morgenthau Plan," which called not only for the summary execution of German leaders but also the deindustrialization of Germany, Roosevelt found it wise, in an election year, to distance himself from Morgenthau, thereby giving Stimson and the War Department an opportunity to fill the war crimes policy vacuum.

The key figure in developing that policy was Lt. Colonel Murray C. Bernays, head of the Special Projects Office of the War Department's Personnel Branch. Bernays proposed that not only Nazi leaders, but also a number of key Nazi organizations, such as the SS and the Gestapo, be tried by an international court for "conspiracy to commit murder, terrorism, and the destruction of peaceful populations in violation of the laws of war."[2] This approach offered a number of important advantages. In addition to providing the opportunity of trying top Nazis for specific offenses under international law, it also made admissible as evidence all acts committed in furtherance of the conspiracy, thus promising to produce a much more complete picture of Nazi crimes than would otherwise be possible. The establishment of the criminal nature of certain Nazi organizations, moreover, would set the stage for the punishment of their members in subsequent proceedings. The British were reluctant to abandon summary execution. But the preference of the Soviet Union and France for trials of some sort, plus the energetic leadership of U.S. Supreme Court Justice Robert H. Jackson, appointed "Chief of Counsel for the Prosecution of Axis Criminality" by President Truman on May 2, 1945, resulted in agreement by the four Allied powers on the conspiracy/criminal organization framework for the trial of major war criminals. This was embodied in the Charter of the International Military Tribunal, signed by representatives of the four powers in London on August 8.[3] Under its terms, the tribunal was to wield authority to try persons who, "either as individuals or as members of organizations," had committed "crimes against peace," (the waging of aggressive war), "war crimes," (violations of the laws and customs of

Exterior of the Nuremberg courthouse. Circa 1945. (NARA)

war), "crimes against humanity," (including the enslavement and extermination of civilian populations), or who had engaged in common plans or conspiracies to commit any of these crimes. With the charter as a legal foundation, the "Trial of Major War Criminals before the International Military Tribunal" would open in Nuremberg on November 20, 1945. The southern German city had been chosen because it contained the only undamaged facility suitable for the trial. That it had also been the scene of the annual Nazi party rallies was a symbolic dividend.

By the fall of 1945, however, the punishment of Germans accused of war crimes had already begun in Germany. Some of this was of a spontaneous, extra-legal nature, reminiscent of earlier recommendations that the war crimes justice problem be solved by summary executions. In the spring of 1945, as advancing Anglo-American ground forces liberated concentration camps, camp prisoners not infrequently vented their fury by killing former tormentors, often with the tacit approval of Allied troops. At Ohrdruf, for example, American soldiers witnessed, without intervening, the beating and stabbing deaths of camp guards, some of whom had

Beaten SS guards. Buchenwald, April 30, 1945.

attempted to escape detection by dressing in civilian clothes. One of the victims was the camp commandant, whose battered body was put on display at the camp entrance. In some instances, prisoners' committees oversaw the administration of summary "justice," which could still be remarkably brutal. At Ebensee, a subcamp of Mauthausen where a mammoth underground armaments complex had been built and operated with appalling loss of life, a particularly savage *Kapo* (a prisoner, often a common criminal, who had been given authority over other prisoners by the SS) was tied to a post in the camp square and slowly beaten to death by over a hundred inmates. Another *Kapo* was allegedly burned alive in the camp crematorium. All told, in excess of 50 persons (solely *Kapos*, as the SS guards had departed at the approach of U.S. troops) were killed. At Bergen-Belsen, entered by British troops in mid-April, random revenge killings were accompanied by the willingness of a prisoners' committee to identify particularly brutal *Kapos* and turn them over to British authorities for later trial.

The only documented example of large-scale participation of Allied troops in revenge killings occurred at Dachau following the liberation of the camp by troops of the U.S. 45th Infantry Division on April 29, 1945. Infuriated by the discovery of a "death train"—39 railway boxcars containing the bodies of thousands of prisoners—and provoked by the initial armed resistance of some SS guards, GIs engaged in an orgy of killing, including lining up SS men and mowing them down with machine-gun fire. Most of the victims were not camp guards, but Waffen SS replacement troops assigned to the defense of the Dachau complex, a major SS training center as well as concentration camp. The number killed is uncertain. An estimate by an American witness of over 500 may be too high; the figure of 21, contained in a report on the incident by the U.S. Seventh Army's inspector general, is certainly too low. These were, in themselves, war crimes, although no GIs were prosecuted for having committed them. That such incidents should have occurred given the horror witnessed by liberating Allied troops and the hatred felt for the SS as a result of well-publicized killings of Allied prisoners of war at their hands is not surprising.

Liberation of the camps aided in the gathering of evidence and the rounding-up of suspects by Allied investigators, and it contributed to the prompt opening of war crimes trials in the Allied occupation zones of Germany. The Trial of Major War Criminals at Nuremberg, which began in November 1945, is by far the best-known trial of Nazi war crimes suspects and was the most significant in regard to the prominence of its defendants and the legal precedents established. But only a tiny fraction (22) of the total number of Germans accused by the Allies of war crimes was tried in that proceeding. It was followed by twelve additional trials held in Nuremberg by the United States under Allied Control Council Law No. 10, sometimes referred to as the "subsequent Nuremberg trials," which lasted until April 1949 (and which inspired the famous 1961 film "Judgment at Nuremberg," starring Spencer Tracy and Burt Lancaster). These proceedings tried a total of 185 "secondary" German leaders, such as industrialists, high-ranking army officers, doctors, and the commanders of *Einsatzgruppen*, the roving SS murder squads that killed more than one million Jews and tens of thousands of Gypsies and Communist leaders in the Soviet Union. By far the largest number of German war crimes defendants was judged by military government courts that were established by the Allies in their zones of occupation, and to these must be added substantial numbers tried by courts held in some of the smaller Allied countries. The United States alone tried 1,672 individuals in 489 such proceedings from 1945 until 1948. General authority for these trials was derived from the Moscow Declaration of

Camp commandant Josef Kramer under guard. Bergen-Belsen, April 17, 1945. (IWM)

November 1, 1943, but it was the long-standing principles set down in the Hague Convention No. IV of 1907 and the Geneva Prisoners of War Convention of 1929 that constituted their specific legal foundation. These statements of the laws of war prohibited the causing of unnecessary harm to combatants and civilians and required that prisoners of war be protected from injury and death.

The first trial to address the operation of concentration camps was opened by the British Army in Lüneburg near Hamburg on September 17, 1945. Although commonly referred to as the "Belsen trial," 12 of its 45 defendants were accused of the killing and ill-treatment of Allied civilians and military personnel at Auschwitz, as well as at Bergen-Belsen. Those on trial ranged from Josef Kramer, who had been commandant of the Auschwitz II (Birkenau) extermination camp for approximately six months and of the Bergen-Belsen concentration camp in the final months of the war, to miscellaneous German guards and functionaries to

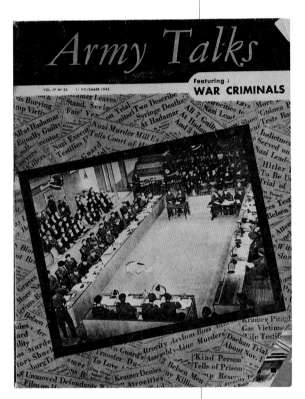

Army Talks, November 11, 1945.
(Henry Eigles Collection, Archives, USHMM)

Kapos, many of them Poles. Observers of the trial were particularly fascinated by Kramer and Irma Grese, a young woman who had served as an SS guard both in Auschwitz and Bergen-Belsen. Kramer was depicted by the news media as a sadistic brute and, with his squat figure and coarse facial features, invited caricature as the gorilla-like "Beast of Belsen." In sharp contrast stood Grese, a strikingly handsome blond-haired, blue-eyed woman in her early twenties, an "angel of death" whose father had whipped her when he learned of her employment in the concentration camps. She, in turn, had allegedly whipped Hungarian Jewish women who had attempted to escape selection for the gas chambers at Auschwitz and had sadistically murdered other prisoners.

As in other war crimes trials, the strict rules of evidence which normally apply in Anglo-American justice were considerably relaxed, permitting the introduction of hearsay evidence. But in most respects, the Belsen trial proceeded much as would an ordinary trial for murder. Each defendant was provided with British defense attorneys who conducted themselves as they were trained to do, attempting to discredit prosecution witnesses and seeking to undermine the credibility of evidence offered against the defendants while, at the same time, trying to put their clients' actions in the most favorable light. For example, defense counsel for Kramer made much of the fact that, on March 1, 1945, his client had written to Richard Glücks, inspector of concentration camps, begging him to refrain from sending additional prisoners from evacuated camps in eastern Europe to horribly overcrowded Belsen, and to provide cooking equipment and medical supplies in order to reduce the camp mortality rate which, due to typhus and malnutrition, had reached 250 to 300 deaths per day. Prosecution witnesses testifying to atrocities committed by other defendants were subjected to vigorous cross-examination on the grounds that they were unable to provide precise times and dates of the crimes they had seen. That one witness may have testified to having seen a prisoner shot in the stomach while another witness recalled seeing the same prisoner shot in the head was seized upon by defense counsel as evidence that prosecution witnesses were lying. Such "lawyerly" behavior, which might have seemed perfectly appropriate in a trial occasioned by a single murder, seemed to many observers grotesquely inappropriate when the dead numbered in the thousands and the survivors had been subjected to almost unimaginable psychological stresses. The magnitude of the crimes for which the defendants were on trial was graphically demonstrated by the courtroom presentation of two films, one made by the British of Belsen and the other by the Russians of Auschwitz. The British film was highly effective in providing visual evidence of the emaciated condition of prisoners and the vast number of corpses discovered when the camp was liberated. Included in the film was the shattering scene of a bulldozer operated by a British soldier pushing a tangled heap of rotting corpses into a mass grave.

At Hadamar, U.S. interrogators question nurse Philomine Ingart about mass slayings. May 4, 1945. (NARA)

While the defendants at the Belsen trial were tried specifically for crimes committed against Allied nationals under the traditional laws of war, the fact that Jews as Jews had suffered disproportionately at their hands was not overlooked. The judge advocate, in his summary of the evidence, asked the court: "Do you think when people have been dragged away to Auschwitz and . . . have been gassed and killed without any trial, because they have committed no crime except that of being a Jew . . . that that is not a clear violation of an unchallenged rule of warfare which outrages the general sentiment of humanity?" And "throughout all these camps the staff were made quite clearly to understand that brutalities [and] ill-treatment . . . would not be punished if they took place at the expense of the Jews, and the case for the Prosecution is that there was this common concerted design to do these horrible and terrible things."[4]

On November 16, the fifty-third day of the trial, the verdicts were handed down. Fourteen of the defendants were acquitted. Of those convicted, eleven—including Kramer and Grese—were sentenced to death by hanging. The remainder were sentenced to terms of imprisonment ranging from one year to life, with the majority in the range of five to fifteen years. Criticism of the Belsen trial was immediate and widespread, both on the grounds of the number of defendants acquitted and the "derisory sentences" imposed on some of those convicted. The French government requested that the fourteen defendants who had been acquitted, including an SS man who had been accused of frequently beating prisoners with a rubber truncheon and having shot two Jewish women dead, be surrendered to French authorities for retrial, but the request was refused by the British War Office.

While the Belsen trial was in progress, the first United States military government court trial for Nazi mass murder opened in Wiesbaden on October 8, 1945. Officially designated "United States vs. Alfons Klein, *et al.*" but more commonly known as the "Hadamar trial," it brought seven defendants accused of crimes committed in the operation of the Hadamar state sanatorium, located in western Germany some five miles from Limburg, before a panel of U.S. Army officers. U.S. Army investigators had gathered evidence indicating that approximately 15,000 mentally ill and handicapped patients had been killed between 1941 and the capture of Hadamar by U.S. forces in March 1945. Today it is known that the institution had broader historical significance, in that many of the killings (justified by the Nazis as "mercy" deaths or so-called euthanasia) had taken place in gas chambers constructed for that purpose at Hadamar and elsewhere, and had served as a "dress rehearsal" for the gassing of Jews in extermination camps.

Although most of the victims of the "Hadamar murder factory" had been Germans, the existing laws of war under which the trial was conducted, which regulated relations between enemies, limited U.S. Army prosecutors, as it had British prosecutors in the Belsen trial, to charging the defendants with crimes against citizens of Allied countries. In the Hadamar case the specific offense alleged was the murder of over 400 tubercular Russian and Polish slave laborers by administering lethal doses of drugs in the last year of the war. Due to the smaller number of defendants and the comparative simplicity of the case, the Hadamar proceeding was much shorter than the Belsen trial, being completed in less than a week. The "trial judge advocate," or chief prosecutor, was Colonel Leon Jaworski, later to gain fame as special prosecutor in the Watergate case. Jaworski had little difficulty in proving that the alleged murders had occurred, since the defendants made no effort to deny them. Instead, with the assistance of German and American defense counsel, the defendants attempted to excuse their conduct on the grounds of superior orders and fear of harsh punishment for disobedience. (The Allies had already agreed to reject the claim of superior orders as a defense in the forthcoming trial of major war criminals and to consider it, at most, as grounds for mitigation of a sentence.) Jaworski was able to demolish the argument by pointing to testimony by Alfons Klein, Hadamar's director, that employees had been free to leave at any time, evidence that Klein's hypocritical claim of superior orders in his own defense did not weaken.

The prosecutions in both the Belsen and Hadamar cases had framed their indictments in the form of conspiracies or common designs to commit mass atrocities, meaning that in principle, all parties were equally guilty. Yet the outcome of the Hadamar trial differed substantially from the British proceeding. All seven of the defendants were found guilty of the charges, and the punishments imposed by the U.S. Army court were much more severe. Three of the defendants, including Klein and two male nurses who had administered fatal doses of drugs on Klein's orders, were sentenced to death by hanging. Dr. Adolf Wahlmann, the elderly chief physician, was given life imprisonment at hard labor, while the remaining defendants received terms at hard labor ranging from 25 to 35 years. The lightest sentence of 25 years at hard labor was imposed on the sole female defendant, a head nurse who had probably passed the names of patients to be killed to the actual murderers. At this stage of the trial program, the U.S. Army could not be faulted for unwarranted leniency.

That impression was strengthened by "U.S. vs. Martin Weiss, *et al.,*" the trial of 40 defendants, all but one former members of the SS, for crimes committed in the operation of Dachau concentration camp, the original "model" for the other concentration camps. Appropriately, the trial was conducted on the grounds of the

"The Silent Jury," *New York Times,*
November 25, 1945.

concentration camp, which was to be the scene of most U.S. military government court trials and an internment center for war crimes suspects and witnesses. The indictment alleged a common design to mistreat Allied nationals, "including killings, beatings, tortures, starvations, abuses and indignities." Among the defendants was Martin Weiss, the second-to-last of Dachau's seven commandants, as well as SS physicians Fritz Hintermeier and Paul Walter, accused of conducting high-altitude experiments on prisoners for the *Luftwaffe.* Dr. Klaus Karl Schilling, the sole civilian defendant, had been professor of parasitology at the University of Berlin and a world-famous authority on tropical diseases. In a vain effort to develop an immunization for malaria, Schilling had infected some 1,200 prisoners with the disease, resulting in death for hundreds. Once again, in comparison with the slow-moving Belsen trial, the U.S. Army proceeded with dispatch and concluded with severity. Chief Prosecutor Lt. Colonel William D. Denson succeeded in approximately one month, from mid-November until mid-December 1945, in securing the convictions of all 40 defendants, and death sentences for 36, including Weiss, Schilling, and Hintermeier. One SS defendant, whom a number of witnesses had praised for acts of kindness towards prisoners, received a life sentence. Remarkably, some surviving inmates of Dachau argued that Weiss should have been spared, due to his "humane" administration of the camp.

By the time the Dachau trial had ended, the centerpiece of the Allied war crimes trial program had opened at Nuremberg. Indictments had been handed down by the four major Allied powers (the United States, Great Britain, the Soviet Union, and France) on October 6, 1945, against 24 defendants and, on November 20, 1945, the trial began. Only 21 defendants were present, for Robert Ley, chief of the German Labor Front, had hanged himself in his cell after expressing remorse for Nazi crimes and, specifically, for those against Jews, while the elderly Gustav

At the Nuremberg IMT, all of the defendants wore headsets that enabled them to hear simultaneous translations of the courtroom proceedings. Hermann Göring used this set.

Krupp of the mammoth German industrial combine, senile and incontinent, had been dropped from the list of defendants (his son, Alfred, would be tried in Case 10 of the subsequent Nuremberg proceedings). Martin Bormann, Hitler's powerful personal secretary and head of the Nazi party chancellery, could not be found (it is now known with virtual certainty that he died attempting to escape from Berlin in the final days of the war), but would be tried *in absentia*. The remaining defendants were a mixed group. Some, such as *Luftwaffe* chief Hermann Göring, armaments minister Albert Speer, and Ernst Kaltenbrunner, second in the ranks of the SS only to Heinrich Himmler (another postwar but unrepentant suicide), were leading figures in the Third Reich, while others were of questionable importance. Notable in the latter category was Hans Fritzsche, a middle-level official in the Nazi propaganda ministry and well-known news broadcaster who had never met Hitler. The fact that he was included among the defendants was a courtesy to the Soviet Union (he was one of the few Nazi officials in Soviet custody).

Individuals were not the only defendants to be tried at Nuremberg. In accordance with the tribunal's charter, six organizations, including the SS, the Gestapo, the leadership corps of the Nazi party, and the supreme command of the German armed forces, were also indicted. This was one of the highly innovative aspects of the Allied case and was without precedent in international law. Other facets of the trial were also novel. Count two of the four-count indictment charged most of the defendants with "crimes against peace," defined as "the planning, preparation,

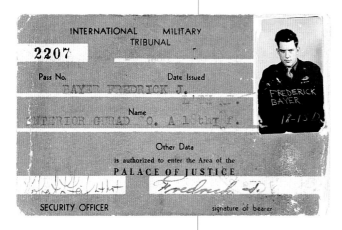

U.S. guard's pass for entry to the Nuremberg courtroom.

(Frederick J. Bayer Papers, Archives, USHMM)

initiation and waging of wars of aggression which were wars in violation of international treaties, agreements and assurances." Although wars fitting that definition had been all-too-common features of international relations over the centuries, never before had they been held to be criminal acts for which national leaders could be tried and punished. Least innovative was count three, under which the majority of defendants was charged with having committed "war crimes." Here, the term simply referred to violations of the traditional and well-established rules of war protecting combatants and civilians from harm not excusable on the grounds of "military necessity." As the Belsen, Hadamar, and Dachau trials had indicated, the traditional rules of war could be made applicable to some of the Nazis' unprecedented atrocities. But it was count four, "crimes against humanity," that specifically addressed the "murder, extermination, enslavement, deportation" of civilian populations "on political, racial or religious grounds." Critics have argued that this, like count two, constituted the creation of *ex post facto* law, that is, holding persons criminally responsible for acts that were not considered criminal at the time when they were committed. But it was the contention of the Allied jurists who had drawn up the indictment that international law is not based solely on treaties and other formal international agreements but is also derived from the evolving sensibilities of "civilized" humanity, which had long recognized in principle the criminality of the offenses committed by the Nazis in fact.

Count one of the indictment was the most problematical. This was the count dealing with conspiracy, by which all of the defendants were charged with having together voluntarily and knowingly planned to wage aggressive war and planned to commit (or order others to commit) war crimes and crimes against humanity. As a separate offense, it was fuzzy and not easy to prove. It was a legal concept, moreover, that was unfamiliar to continental, including German, law. Both the defendants and their attorneys (at Nuremberg, exclusively German) had difficulty understanding it, and the Allied judges would find themselves badly divided over this count in their final deliberations.[5]

SS gathering up captured documents presented as evidence before the IMT. Nuremberg, Fall 1945. (NARA)

The trial before the International Military Tribunal lasted approximately ten months. It was a trial awash in paper. U.S. Supreme Court Justice Robert Jackson, the American chief prosecutor, persuaded the prosecution that the Allied case should be based primarily on documentary evidence. He argued that this would be a far more effective means of demonstrating the guilt of men who had ordered criminal acts than the testimony of witnesses and would, at the same time, produce an irrefutable record of Nazi criminality. The tribunal's documentation division evaluated about 100,000 captured German documents and offered some 4,000 of these in evidence. Employed in the sorting and filing of these documents, ironically, were former Waffen SS men from a nearby prisoner-of-war camp. But the dependence on documentary evidence produced a number of problems. American prosecutors deluged the court with documents which they themselves did not always understand and, in the process, bored and confused not only the press but the judges as well. And although prosecution documents were supposed to be made available to the defense, this was not always done in a timely fashion. More importantly, documents failed to convey adequately the dimensions of human suffering caused by Nazi criminality. Although the American prosecution

The 21 Nuremberg defendants seated in the dock. Rear row left to right: Karl Dönitz, Erich Raeder, Baldur von Schirach, Fritz Sauckel, Alfred Jodl, Franz von Papen, Arthur Seyss-Inquart, Albert Speer, Constantin von Neurath, and Hans Fritzsche. Front row: Hermann Göring, Rudolph Hess, Joachim von Ribbentrop, Wilhelm Keitel, Ernest Kaltenbrunner, Alfred Rosenberg, Hans Frank, Julius Streicher, Walter Funk, and Hjalmar Schacht. (NARA)

team presented evidence on December 14, 1945, that 6,000,000 Jews had been murdered by the Nazis, it could not compare in its effect to the later testimony (surprisingly, for the defense) of Rudolf Höss, first commandant of Auschwitz. A German attorney recalled that "[Höss's words] rained blood, one breathed ashes, the smell of burned corpses poisoned the atmosphere."[6]

As the International Military Tribunal adjourned on December 20, 1945, for a two-week holiday, it had barely begun the enormous task of hearing and sifting evidence. Most of the trial was to unfold in 1946, and would conclude on September 30 with the handing down of verdicts and sentencing of those convicted.

Three defendants (news broadcaster Fritzsche, former Vice-Chancellor and Ambassador Franz von Papen, and ex-economics minister and banker Hjalmar Schacht) were acquitted. Of the convicted, twelve, including Bormann *in absentia,* were sentenced to death by hanging. Ten of the sentences were carried out in the pre-dawn hours of October 16. Göring escaped the hangman by committing suicide in his cell with a cyanide capsule, possibly concealed in a meerschaum pipe. The remaining convicted prisoners received prison terms of ten years to life. Deputy Führer Rudolf Hess, the last of the Nuremberg convicts, died in Berlin's Spandau prison in August 1987. Of the six organizations indicted along with the individual defendants, three, including the SS, the Gestapo-SD, and the "leadership corps" of the Nazi party, were held to have been criminal. Membership in these organizations, particularly the SS, would serve as a charge in some of the subsequent trials.

Anglo-American war crimes trials continued through 1949 and executions were carried out well into 1951. But enthusiasm for continuing the program was on the wane by 1949. The beginning of the Cold War and the determination of the United States to "contain" Communism quickly converted Germans in the western zones of occupation from defeated enemies into potential allies against the Soviet Union. War crimes trials, unpopular among many Germans, seemed an obstacle to cooperation. Questions about the correctness of judicial procedures followed in certain lesser trials, some of them legitimate, combined with political expediency and simple fatigue to bring the trial program to an end. Yet international law had undergone one of the most important extensions in its history, although the tangible benefits of that development have so far been modest.

1. Bradley F. Smith, *The American Road to Nuremberg: The Documentary Record, 1944–1945* (Stanford, 1982), 13–14.
2. Ibid., 36.
3. Office of the United States Chief of Counsel for Prosecution of Axis Criminality, *Nazi Conspiracy and Aggression* (Washington, 1948), 1:5.
5. Raymond Phillips, ed., *Trial of Josef Kramer and Forty-four Others (The Belsen Trial)* (London, 1949), 632, 639–40.
6. For the text of the indictment, see *Nazi Conspiracy and Aggression* 1:13–56.
7. Robert Conot, *Justice at Nuremberg* (New York, 1983), 376.

JAMES J. WEINGARTNER is Professor of History at the Southern Illinois University at Edwardsville. He is author of *Hitler's Guard: The Story of the Leibstandarte SS Adolf Hitler, 1933–1945* (Southern Illinois University Press, 1974) and *Crossroads of Death: The Story of the Malmedy Massacre and Trial* (University of California Press, 1979). His many articles include "Comprehending Mass Murder: The Buchenwald Trial of 1947," in *The Midwest Quarterly* 30 (Winter 1989).

A CONTINENT IN CHAOS: EUROPE AND THE DISPLACED PERSONS

Jewish refugees arrive at the Zeilsheim displaced
persons camp. Germany, 1945–46.
(Alice Robinson Lev Collection, Photo Archive, USHMM)

The International Tracing Service (ITS) in Arolsen, Germany,
assisted survivors in locating lost relatives. February 1946.
(Ghetto Fighters' House, Kibbutz Lohamei ha-Ghettaot, Israel)

Polish Jews who found safe haven at a DP
center in the American zone of occupied
Germany. Berlin, Germany, January 24, 1946.

(Bettmann Archive, New York)

Displaced persons (in white shirts) serve on a
judicial panel in a trial about the sale of an ID card
by a fellow DP at Feldafing, Germany. 1945.
(Collection of Helen Tichauer, New York)

President Truman's envoy, Earl G. Harrison (sixth
from left), visits the Bergen-Belsen DP camp. July 1945.

(Yad Vashem, Jerusalem, Israel)

Zionist protesters from the Landsberg DP camp.

November 15, 1945.

(Irving Heymont Collection, American Jewish Archives, Cincinnati)

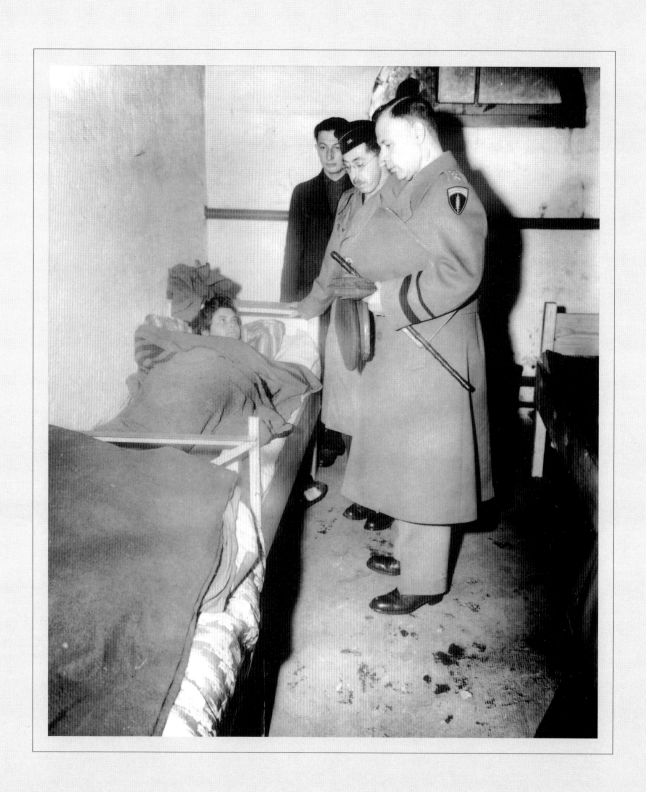

Lt. Gen. Walter Bedell Smith, Chief of Staff of U.S. forces in the European Theater (holding cap), and Judge Samuel H. Rifkind, the Army's advisor on Jewish affairs, inspect living conditions at Landsberg. December 6, 1945. (NARA)

Abraham J. Peck

Displaced persons leave camp at Bamberg, Germany. July 11, 1945.
(David Scherman, LIFE Magazine © Time, Inc.)

Long, long lines. That is what Europe's displaced millions remembered about the first days and weeks following the surrender of Nazi Germany on May 8, 1945. Endless lines of weary, ill-clothed, and confused Europeans marching past destroyed German and Austrian towns and cities, often several hundreds of miles from their own places of birth. While they could see the devastation around them, they had little time to reflect on what it meant. They knew only that the terrible conflict that had left a continent in ruins was finally over. It was time to go home.

Most estimates put the number of homeless and uprooted people wandering throughout Central Europe in the spring of 1945 at eleven million. Seven million of them were on German soil. Among them were foreign nationals who had willingly come to Nazi Germany to work for the Third Reich; some, including many Poles, were former conscripted laborers; others were inmates from concentration, forced labor, and prisoner-of-war camps. And there were the small number of Jews who had survived camp internment and death marches at the very end of the war.

Dutch DPs await transportation home. Bamberg, Germany, July 11, 1945.
(David Scherman, LIFE Magazine © Time, Inc.)

ALLIED PLANS FOR DISPLACED PERSONS

The Allies and the refugee organization, the United Nations Relief and Rehabilitation Administration (UNRRA), classified as "displaced persons" (DPs) the millions of non-German and non-Austrian nationals. As early as 1943 the western Allies had begun to prepare for the end of the war and a time when the DPs would need care. In November 1943 UNRRA was chartered and assumed the task of training teams of workers to administer DP "assembly centers" and to help the military with the huge task of repatriation. Yet the organization remained subservient to SHAEF (Supreme Headquarters Allied Expeditionary Force)—the Allied command which had led the invasion of Germany—until the end of 1945.

Numerous memoranda issued by SHAEF in late 1944 and early 1945 defined the various categories of displaced persons and the role of military authorities in caring for these DPs. Thus, SHAEF gave the military government in occupied zones the authority to determine those persons of former enemy nationality "persecuted because of their race, religion, or activities in favor of the United Nations" and to treat such persecuted or "stateless" persons as UNDPs. SHAEF could designate DPs as "non-repatriable" and was charged with accommodating such persons in separate assembly centers "selected, equipped, and staffed with a view to relatively permanent occupation." UNDPs would not be billeted by the German population, but written policy stated that German residences would "as necessary be requisitioned, vacated and used to provide accommodation."

Despite these careful preparations, the Allied military forces who carved Germany and Austria into zones of occupation failed in the first few months of occupation to identify non-repatriable persons and provide them with the care to which they were entitled. As one historian has commented, "On paper the organizational plans seemed impressive but, especially at the beginning, almost nothing worked out as planned."[1]

Liberated prisoners return to Lidice, Czechoslovakia, 1945.
(SOVFOTO, New York)

ALLIED EXPEDITIONARY FORCE

D. P. INDEX CARD

B 00179940

1. (Registration number)   16—35306-1

2. (Family name)   (Other given names)

3. (Signature of holder)   D.P.1

Supreme Headquarters Allied Expeditionary Force (SHAEF) index card used to establish DP status. (Kurt Moses Collection)

In practice, the Allied military authorities had little time to determine which DPs were non-repatriable, especially if it involved (as it often did) the necessity of filling out a duplicate of the pre-printed form "A.E.F. DP Registration Record" and forwarding it to SHAEF for review. The military's overriding goal after liberation was to repatriate as many foreign nationals under its administration as possible. The Allies did, in fact, repatriate with great energy and resourcefulness millions of non-German Europeans in the months between May and September 1945.

For those repatriated, it was often a time of great joy and celebration. Trainloads of western European repatriates traveled along the devastated German countryside. There was singing and cheering; signs adorned the sides of the trains announcing which nationality was on board and where they were heading.

Jewish orphans from Buchenwald prepare to leave Germany in early June 1945. (NARA)

But other DPs were not so eager to return. Soviet DPs, many of them former prisoners of war, were not certain what kind of response they would receive upon their return to the Soviet Union. Stories circulated that instead of being greeted as war heroes, great numbers of Soviet returnees had been put on trial and executed.

But most Soviet DPs had little choice in the matter. The great majority had been willingly or unwillingly repatriated by September 1945 in accordance with a repatriation agreement signed by the Soviet Union, the United States, and Great Britain. The American military did not like to impose forcible repatriation. It only went after Soviet soldiers who had been in German uniforms, such as the notorious General Vlasov, a renegade Soviet general who had turned the troops under his command against the Red Army and fought with the German Army.

NON-REPATRIABLES

Hundreds of thousands of Polish DPs also did not wish to return home. Some were fearful of the Soviet presence in Poland and what that meant for the nation's political future. But the vast majority simply did not like their chances in a nation devastated by nearly six years of total war fought on its soil. In the summer and fall of 1945, the American, British, and French had nearly 800,000 Polish non-repatriables living in their zones of occupied Germany and Austria.

Another group of DPs not eager to return were thousands of eastern Europeans from the Baltic nations of Latvia, Lithuania, and Estonia. Along with many Ukrainians, they were the least eager of the European nationals who had the opportunity to return home. Many of them did not want to return to countries controlled by the Soviet Union. They would come back only with arms to free their homelands from the yoke of communism. Other Balts, however, along with the Ukrainians, refused to be repatriated because they had collaborated with the Nazis and feared retribution upon their return. A number of the Ukrainians had been concentration camp guards, some in the killing centers. By the fall of 1945, about 150,000 to 200,000 Balts and Ukrainians remained in the western occupied zones.

DISPLACED CHILDREN

The most heartbreaking group of DPs were the children. The International Red Cross estimated that 13 million children in Europe had lost their parents and siblings. UNRRA gave medical and psychological care to 50,000 unaccompanied children in the months after liberation in a number of special DP centers for children.

Russian children, April 1945.

(William Vandivert, LIFE Magazine © Time, Inc.)

Everywhere the Allies liberated human beings from the depths of their physical and spiritual degradation, there too were children: "the 700 children 'almost like wild animals,' discovered in the prisons of Lodz, Poland; half-starved youngsters wandering in the woods of eastern Slovakia; youthful beggars filling Athens and Rome; young searchers everywhere seeking news of their families from travelers and released prisoners of war."[2]

"Homeless, scarred, bitter, fearful, gaunt, robbing, witnesses to terrible things—these were the children of liberated Europe," is how one historian has described the youngest of the European DPs. Some children had been taken to Germany to be used as slave labor; some had even been made to fight in the German army during the last weeks of the war. Others had been abducted from their parents and brought to Germany to be "Aryanized" and raised in German families.

When they were freed from Nazi bondage, many were on the verge of total exhaustion or worse. Thirty Polish girls who had worked on Nazi farms were brought, after liberation, to an UNRRA children's center near Dachau. This is how they were described:

> Most of them were in rags, all showed marked effects of malnutrition and mental anxiety. Their hair was a mat filled with lice. All had skin infections, two so seriously that they were unable to wear shoes. Their feet and legs were wrapped in dirty blood-stained gauze. Some were so confused that they thought themselves German.[3]

One American GI described meeting a 12-year-old survivor:

> It is the first child to go through this hell that I have seen. And what a sight. He looks normal enough in size and otherwise until you look at his eyes. These look as if they belonged to a man of 70. And he talks like one—the seriousness and resignation of an old man. . . . He wasn't like a boy at all. I felt like a kid beside him.[4]

More than one million Jewish children were murdered during the Holocaust. The Jewish children who survived included those hidden by Christian families while many of the children's parents had perished in Nazi camps. Some children had been left in Catholic monasteries and cared for by priests and nuns. Often the children had been baptized as Christians for their own protection, and sometimes because it was part of the Church's mandate to save Jewish souls. Whether the children would be returned to Jewish authority was never guaranteed. Some of those who were returned to Jewish identity went to Switzerland, France, and Sweden after the war, and from there, often to Palestine.

DP CAMPS

When it became evident that more than one million DPs were to remain unrepatriable in 1945, SHAEF was ill prepared to care for them. The military viewed its main task as keeping order and carrying out its occupation of Germany and

Identity card for Jacques Danner, a Jehovah's Witness who was imprisoned in a concentration camp.
(Gift of Ruth Danner, Collections, USHMM)

Austria. Yet throughout 1945, UNRRA also proved incapable of caring adequately for the needs of unrepatriable DPs. UNRRA teams that in theory were supposed to have at least 13 members per unit often had six or fewer. Supplies were limited and the DPs were constantly upset over the number of calories allowed them per day (often considerably less than 2,000).

The non-repatriables were provided housing in former German army barracks, prisoner-of-war camps, concentration camps such as Bergen-Belsen and Dachau, garages, stalls, hospitals, sanatoria, and the like. There were nearly 900 assembly centers with populations ranging in size from 50 to 7,000 inhabitants, and conditions varied considerably from place to place. In many, however, conditions were poor.

Liberated camp prisoners loot food and supplies in Munich. April 30, 1945. (NARA)

Many of the DP camps were surrounded with barbed wire and armed guards as part of the military's efforts to maintain control of the large DP population. Keeping order in postwar Germany meant keeping in check such illegal activities as looting and black marketeering. After liberation, many DPs and Germans had plundered stores and depots in cities like Munich; many DPs had suffered terribly at the hands of the Nazi regime and had been determined, through looting, to exact a measure of revenge against Germany and the Germans.

The DP centers had mixed populations, with peoples of all European nationalities, languages, and religions thrown together. Those DPs who had collaborated with the Nazis often shared centers with victims of Nazi persecution, exacerbating already existing hatreds.

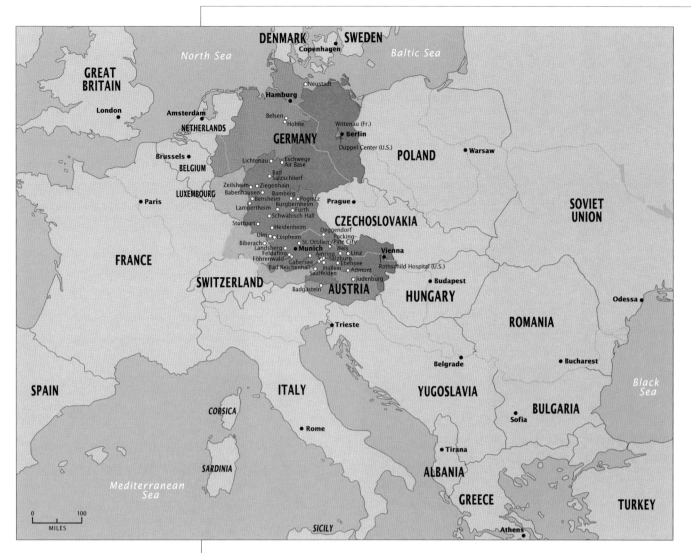

Major Jewish DP Assembly Centers, 1945–1946

Zones of Occupation:
British
French
U.S.
Soviet

Principal source: *Summary of D.P. Population: UNRRA Assembly Centers in the United States Zone (Washington, D.C., 1946).*

THE PLIGHT OF JEWISH DPS

Perhaps the unhappiest of the DP groups were the Jews. Each day after liberation only brought more horrible news about the fate of Jewish life under the Nazis. Beyond the incredible numbers of Jews murdered, which soon was known to approach six million, was the realization that a thousand-year-old Jewish civilization in central and eastern Europe was no more. Entire towns and villages which had once contained thriving Jewish communities had been totally destroyed.

But for most of the Jews in the assembly centers of Germany and Austria (and a far smaller number in Italy), such realizations would have to wait. More important was the whereabouts of a father, of a mother, a brother or a sister. Some Jews decided to go back to Poland and other parts of eastern Europe and actively search for their families. Others relied on informal networks to seek the information they hoped would tell them that someone dear to them had survived.

The Jewish inhabitants of the assembly centers stayed close to each other. This was also true of the various nationalities in the same centers. A Pole stayed with other Poles, a Lithuanian with other Lithuanians, a Ukrainian with other Ukrainians. But UNRRA workers in the camps could not help notice that the Jewish situation was different. Jews from Poland, Lithuania, the Ukraine, it did not matter:

they all remained together. Some of the UNRRA workers noted that the greatest hardship of the Jewish DPs in their care was having to share the camps with Nazi collaborators and former enemy prisoners of war. They suggested turning some of the centers into "all-Jewish camps."

The Allied military commanders, however, were generally opposed to such an idea. They were determined not to imitate the actions of the Nazis in classifying

An UNRRA official records statistics on DP camp populations near Klagenfurt, Germany. December 14, 1945. (FPG International, New York)

Insignia patch worn by United Nations Relief and Rehabilitation Administration workers. (Kevin Mahoney Collection)

people by religion or race. Rabbi Abraham J. Klausner, an American military chaplain, remembered an encounter with a military officer in the spring of 1945. He had gone to plead the case of Jewish DPs in one assembly center who wished to be separated from the other DPs, a number of whom were known to be vicious antisemites and Nazi collaborators. After listening to Klausner, the American officer in charge replied, "I don't know what you are talking about. There are no Jews in this camp!" Klausner, stunned at the officer's answer, mentioned that he had just held a meeting with several dozen Jews next door to the building in which he and the officer were standing. The officer shouted at the top of his voice: "I told you that there are no Jews in this camp. Look at the chart behind me. Do you see any Jews?" The chart in question was a breakdown of the nationalities living in the camp. There was indeed no such separate listing of Jews.

Allied military neutrality on the "special treatment" of Jews took the policy to often ridiculous extremes. Italian, German, Austrian, and Hungarian Jews—in other words, many Jews from former enemy nations—received no special treatment (such as the higher rations that written policy accorded victims of Nazi persecution), even though many of them had been rounded up by their fellow countrymen, shipped to Nazi concentration camps and killing centers, and murdered by the hundreds of thousands. It would be many months until all Jews, regardless of nation of origin, would receive greater supplies of food rations than enemy nationals.

Yet it was not only in official military circles that the request of Jewish DPs to be shown special treatment was viewed negatively. Regular enlisted men, too, showed signs of irritation with the Jews. During the summer of 1945, many battle-weary veterans of the last great drive against the Germans, including the discovery of the concentration camps, began to leave Germany for the Pacific war or to go stateside. Replacing them were new troops who had not seen the horrors of the camps. What these new soldiers saw were frequently unkempt, poorly dressed, often depressed Jewish survivors, whom they compared unfavorably to the well-dressed, middle-class German women and children they encountered.

The GI also saw the other non-repatriables in the camps, the Poles and Balts, who seemed so healthy and orderly and well-behaved. No wonder that American soldiers did not easily sympathize with the special plight of the Jewish DPs. If the Jews did not like the way the assembly centers were set up, "let them go back where they came from."[5]

Of the more than one million non-repatriables in Germany and Austria in the fall of 1945, there were perhaps 50,000 Jewish survivors. While they were an insignificant percentage of those in the assembly centers, their plight, however, did not go unnoticed, particularly by the few American Jewish military chaplains who ostensibly were in Germany and Austria to provide for the spiritual needs of the troops. Most of the chaplains found ways of helping the Jews in the assembly centers with food, clothing, and information about relatives in the United States. One chaplain in particular, Rabbi Abraham J. Klausner, did whatever it took to make the lives of the survivors easier. He organized lists of survivors and distributed them to the assembly centers; he created hospitals to treat the most critically ill Jews; he pushed for the right of the Jewish survivors to obtain their own camps. Because he sometimes daringly departed from military regulations to get his job done, Klausner was nearly court-martialed on several occasions.[6]

Jewish DPs at Bergen-Belsen protest their continued confinement in the camp. Fall 1945.
(YIVO Institute for Jewish Research, New York)

The major Jewish relief agency, the American Jewish Joint Distribution Committee ("the Joint"), and other Jewish organizations were seriously handicapped in their ability to assist Jewish DPs in 1945 because Allied military authorities did not want them in Germany or Austria. The Allied occupation forces wanted to repatriate all DPs, including Jews, as quickly as possible. Organizations like the Joint could potentially make a temporary situation permanent. Only in late summer 1945 did Joint teams start arriving in the American, British, and French zones to begin the job of providing real assistance to the Jewish survivors, and they continued to be hindered in providing supplies because of military restrictions on transatlantic shipping.[7]

THE HARRISON INVESTIGATION OF DP CAMPS

The plight of Jews in the DP camps also caught the eye of journalists, American officials, and American Jewish leaders. On July 21, the World Jewish Congress (WJC) appealed to Allied leaders meeting at Potsdam to release the former camp inmates from "conditions of the most abject misery." The WJC charged that Jews in the Lingen DP camp were housed in "indescribably filthy" structures, with inadequate medical and other supplies and personnel.[8]

Jewish DPs who survived Buchenwald and Mauthausen concentration camps return to eastern Europe. 1945. (IWM)

More important, officials in the American government were contacted by numerous leaders from the American Jewish community about the plight of Jewish survivors, and they sought to inform President Harry S Truman. President Truman, obviously under the influence of the American military, was not entirely sympathetic. He refused to create a commission to deal with the plight of the DPs that had been proposed by Henry Morgenthau, Jr. But Morgenthau was not easily dissuaded. After all, he had been responsible for the creation of the War Refugee Board in 1944, a body which had saved thousands of Europe's Jews. Morgenthau found an ally in Joseph Grew, acting secretary of the Department of State, who appointed Earl G. Harrison, an attorney and the dean of the University of Pennsylvania Law School, to survey the conditions in the DP camps and to submit a detailed report on the condition of displaced persons, "especially the Jews." On June 21, 1945, Grew notified Truman that the State Department had chosen Harrison to lead an investigation of the DP camps. Grew urged Truman to give Harrison "an expression of your interest [which] will facilitate the mission and reassure interested groups concerned with the future of the refugees. . . ." Truman did this in a letter to Harrison dated June 22.

No one could have known just how correct and how important the choice of Earl G. Harrison was for the Jews in occupied Germany and Austria. Harrison had been the director of Alien Registration at the U.S. Department of Justice and served as the U.S. Commissioner of Immigration and Naturalization between 1942 and 1944. He had a tremendous degree of sympathy and understanding for the plight of stateless and homeless human beings.

Harrison arrived in Germany in July. At the same time, Abraham Klausner had discussed his visit with a contact in the SHAEF command. It became obvious to Klausner that the American military had prepared an itinerary for Harrison that would allow him to see only what it wanted him to see. Klausner arranged a meeting with Harrison at a hotel in Munich and presented him with an alternative itinerary, one that would show the real plight of the Jewish survivors.[9] While no documentary evidence exists to support this meeting, Harrison undoubtedly saw Jewish life in the DP camps at its worst.

Harrison visited 30 camps in the American zones of Germany and Austria as well as the Bergen-Belsen/Hohne camp in the British zone of Germany. What he saw and heard "outraged him." One historian has summarized what Harrison and those who accompanied him found in the camps:

> They found 14,000 DPs at Wildflecken under heavy guard. Jews in Celle living in horse stalls, and 14,000 DPs still in the old concentration camp buildings in Bergen-Belsen. . . . Several military officials with whom they spoke expressed the view that "maybe Hitler had something with reference to the Jews."[10]

A Jewish inhabitant of the Bergen-Belsen camp remembered Harrison, who chain-smoked cigarettes as tears streamed down his face. "He was so shaken he could not speak," the Belsen DP recalled. Finally, Harrison whispered in a weak voice "But how did you survive, and where do you take your strength from now?"[11]

By August 1, Harrison had already sent two interim reports offering some of his findings to Grew and to Secretary of the Treasury Fred Vinson. On August 3, General Eisenhower received a summary of Harrison's report. Eisenhower was not pleased.

What did the Harrison report conclude about the conditions of the Jewish DPs? Section II of the report was titled "Needs of the Jews." It began with a very direct criticism of the military's policy concerning the non-recognition of Jews as a national group:

> The first and plainest need of these people is their recognition as Jews. . . . Most of them have spent years in . . . the concentration camps. . . . Jews as Jews have been more severely victimized than the non-Jewish members of the same or other nationalities.[12]

"'Attend unto My Cry!'" St. Louis Post-Dispatch, December 19, 1945.

Harrison then went on to describe the needs of the Jews in great detail, including the need for their own camps and stressing their desire to leave Germany and

Austria for Palestine. But the most devastating part of his report sent tremors through the American military and was the cause of great anger and resentment:

> As matters now stand, we appear to be treating the Jews as the Nazis treated them, except that we do not exterminate them. They are in concentration camps in large numbers under military guard instead of SS troops. One is led to wonder whether the German people, seeing this, are not supposing that we are following or at least condoning Nazi policy.[13]

When President Truman received the report, he immediately told Eisenhower to fix the situation. Eisenhower, in turn, appointed Rabbi Judah Nadich as his adviser on Jewish affairs. He also ordered the creation of separate Jewish DP camps and the requisition of German homes for use by Jewish DPs. He also increased the number of calories allowed them. He did this all the while denying many of Harrison's allegations, especially the comparison of American policy towards the Jews with that of the Nazis.[14]

By the end of 1945, at least 12 camps in the American zone were entirely Jewish. Landsberg and Föhrenwald housed about 5,000 Jews each, and Feldafing, which with the help of Rabbi Klausner had become an all-Jewish camp even before the Harrison report was made public, had about 3,700. In the British zone, Bergen-Belsen/Hohne had about 9,500 Jewish inhabitants. UNRRA assumed operation of the camps on November 15, but the military was still the final arbiter on most matters, including lodging, security, and the supplies of food and clothing. In mid-November, the British zone approved the segregation of Jews within their camps, while stubbornly insisting that "special camps exclusively for Jews will not be established."

LIFE IN THE JEWISH DP CAMPS

A separate Jewish existence in the occupied zones of Germany and Austria had begun. Finally, as 1945 drew to an end, some sense of who they were and what they wanted became clear to the Jewish DPs. It was as if they were living in one vast Jewish cemetery with no hope of leaving its confines. Entry to Palestine was blocked by British fears of Arab hostility; emigration to the United States and other nations was made extremely difficult by unyielding quota systems. Yet despair was overcome by hope. Instead of allowing themselves to be overwhelmed by blocked immigration, overcrowded housing, and the knowledge that the tragedy they had just endured destroyed most of their families and friends, the Jewish DPs resolved to create a new beginning.

Displaced persons repair shoes at Feldafing, the first Jewish DP camp. 1945. (AP/Wide World Photos, New York)

With the growing support of Jewish and international relief organizations, the Jewish camps slowly became centers of Jewish cultural life. Secular schools provided a curriculum based on the highly successful *Tarbut* (Hebrew for "culture") schools in prewar Poland. Dozens of camp newspapers were published. Camp theaters and musical groups were organized. The development and continuity of religious life was supported by American and British rabbis, who served as sources of spiritual comfort.

Political parties were formed in the camps by the end of 1945, mirroring the various Zionist philosophies and groups then active in Palestine and elsewhere. The political slates that ran against each other in camp elections were distinguished not only by varying Zionist philosophies but also by the geographic backgrounds of the candidates. In one camp Polish Jews predominated; in another, Jews from Lithuania.

The Landsberg camp, especially, became a kind of "model" for Jewish camps in the American zone. This was due in no small measure to the efforts of Major Irving Heymont, the 27-year-old American officer who ran the camp from August until December 1945. Heymont was a career military officer who did things "by the book," so much so that he hid the fact that he was a Jew so as not to influence his relationship to the DPs. But his compassion and caring were also a part of his character, and he brought a measure of democracy and independence to Landsberg that was the envy of other camps.

The survivors themselves began to organize simultaneously on a local and zonal level. Here Rabbi Abraham Klausner, again, played an extraordinary role, helping to create the Central Committee of Liberated Jews in the American Zone of Germany. The Committee's first head was Dr. Zalman Grinberg, an articulate and charismatic physician from Lithuania. Dr. Samuel Gringauz, who was head of the Landsberg DP committee, was also an important figure; in 1947 and 1948,

A Jewish double wedding at Feldafing, Germany. Fall 1945.

(Alexander Ferson Collection, Sydney, Australia)

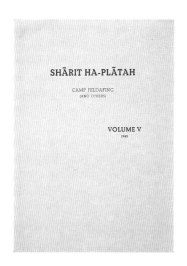

SHĀRIT HA-PLĀTAH

CAMP FELDAFING
(AND OTHERS)

VOLUME V
1945

Volumes of *Sharit Ha-Platah* ("surviving remnant") listed names of concentration camp survivors. 1945.

(Rabbi Abraham Klausner Collection)

Gringauz would write a number of brilliant essays crystallizing the mission sur- survivors sought to carry out as the *Sharit Ha-Platah* (Hebrew for the "surviving remnant").[15]

The Jewish DPs in the British zone at the Bergen-Belson/ Hohne DP camp also began to organize. They were led by Joseph (Yosele) Rosensaft and his wife, Hadassah Bimko-Rosensaft, as well as by Norbert Wollheim, a German Jew formerly from Berlin. Bergen-Belsen was notable for its excellent newspaper, the first of the Jewish press to be founded, and for its excellent theater. There was a closeness among the Jewish DPs in Bergen-Belsen that was to be found nowhere else, a closeness these survivors still share to the present day.

The Jewish DP camps began to grow dramatically at the end of 1945 due to the ongoing acts of antisemitism against Jews in Poland and other parts of eastern Europe. In 1945 alone, after the German surrender, more than 400 Polish Jews were killed in acts of violence. More and more Jews began to leave Poland, Romania, and other countries and try to make their way illegally into the American and British zones and en route to Palestine. They were aided by the *Brichah* (Hebrew for "flight"), a clandestine organization of Palestinian and other Jews, and by the non-interference of the American military which had begun to lose its resentful attitude toward the Jewish DPs.

The Jewish DP camps became home to nearly 250,000 Jews before most of them closed by 1952. One camp, Föhrenwald, would come under the control of the Federal Republic of Germany in 1952 and not close until the beginning of 1957.

This menorah made from spent cartridges and scraps was used at a Hanukkah celebration in Bergen-Belsen.

(Sadie Hofstein, Director of Children's House, Bergen-Belsen Displaced Persons Camp, May 1945–March 1946)

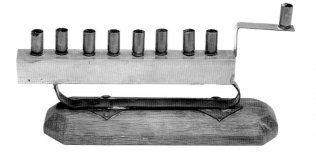

The insensitivity of a world that had not yet absorbed the lessons of the Holocaust kept some Jews waiting in DP camps for many years. Finally, in 1948, the state of Israel was born, and the camps began to empty. With Israel as a safety valve for the Jewish DPs, the flow out of the camps by all DPs moved quickly; England, Canada, Australia, and the South American nations also made provisions to accept significant numbers, mostly Christians.

CONCLUSION

The months between April and December 1945, such a short period of time, had seen the rebirth of a continent and the scattered remnant of a nearly destroyed people. They were months of chaos and confusion, marked by the actions of noble and not so noble human beings. Europe was starting anew, but it would do so without the presence of millions of its Jewish inhabitants who lay in countless, unmarked graves, the victims of a continent and a world gone mad.

In the Feldafing camp, one DP, Simon Schochet, was preparing to leave for America:

> I visit with all my friends and talk with them until late into the night. . . . I look at all the people I have known, as if to keep their stories and faces fixed in my mind so that I can summon their memory in future uncertain times.
>
> I think about what this summer will be like in Feldafing after I am gone. Or will it even matter to me when I am in far off America? . . . Will [my friends] seem like part of a great impressionistic canvas, obscured in the blurred filter of my memories and dreams?
>
> I look out at Feldafing, at the barracks, villas, woods and lake. One day it will again become a peaceful town swarming with happy people. . . . The present inhabitants will be forgotten and dispersed throughout the world. Are the happiness and sorrows experienced here to vanish without an impact?[16]

It is hoped that the happiness and sorrows of liberated Europe in 1945 will indeed be remembered.

Abraham Peck with his father, Shalom, and mother, Anna, at the Landsberg DP camp. 1948. (Abraham Peck Collection)

This essay is dedicated to my father, Shalom W. Peck and to the blessed memory of my mother, Anna Kolton Peck. They both lived in the Landsberg DP camp from August 1945 until November 1949. It is their story as well.

1. Otto B. Burianek, Jr., "The U.S. Army and Displaced Persons in Munich in 1945," unpublished paper in possession of author; Leonard Dinnerstein, *America and the Survivors of the Holocaust* (New York, 1982), 11.
2. Mark Wyman, *DP: Europe's Displaced Persons, 1945–1951* (Philadelphia, 1989), 86, citing Dorothy Macardle, *Children of Europe—A Study of the Children of Liberated Countries: Their War-Time Experiences, Their Reactions, and Their Needs, with a Note on Germany* (Boston, 1951), 79, 244.
3. Zlato Balokovic, "A Nation Cares for Its Own," *The Child*, July 1946, 26; cited by Wyman, *DP*, 88.
4. Akiva Skidell, "Letters from a Jewish Soldier in the American Army: Europe, September 1944–December 1945," unpublished manuscript in possession of author, 60 (entry of May 18).

5. Displaced Persons Report No. September, Appendix A, 3; Combined Displaced Persons Executive, R-Andre 463, CAD 1945, Box 212, National Archives; Dinnerstein, *Survivors*, 56.

6. On Klausner, see Alex Grobman, *Rekindling the Flame. American Jewish Chaplains and the Survivors of European Jewry, 1944–1948* (Detroit, 1993).

7. Yehuda Bauer, *Out of the Ashes. The Impact of American Jews on Post-Holocaust European Jewry* (Oxford, 1989).

8. Angelika Königseder and Juliane Wetzel, *Lebensmut im Wartesaal. Die jüdischen DPs (Displaced Persons) im Nachkriegsdeutschland* (Frankfurt am Main, 1994), 135.

9. Interview with Rabbi Abraham J. Klausner, May 13, 1991, American Jewish Archives, Cincinnati, Ohio.

10. Dinnerstein, *Survivors*, 40.

11. Quoted in Wyman, *DP*, 135.

12. *Report of Earl G. Harrison: Mission to Europe to inquire into the condition and needs of those among the displaced persons in the liberated countries of Western Europe and in the SHAEF area of Germany, with particular reference to the Jewish refugees who may possibly be stateless or non-repatriable* (Washington, 1945), 5.

13. Ibid., 9.

14. Betsy Hill Khalili, "American Policy and the Jewish Displaced Persons: The Harrison Report, August 1945," M.A. thesis, University of Missouri, Kansas City, 1990; Timothy A. Brody, "Earl G. Harrison, Displaced Jews, and the Palestine Question," Honors thesis, Dartmouth College, 1990.

15. See Abraham J. Peck, "Jewish Survivors of the Holocaust in Germany: Revolutionary Vanguard or Remnants of a Destroyed People?" *Tel Aviver Jahrbuch für Deutsche Geschichte* 19 (1990): 33–45.

16. Simon Schochet, *Feldafing* (Vancouver, 1983), 174–75.

ABRAHAM J. PECK is the Administrative Director of the American Jewish Archives of the Hebrew Union College-Jewish Institute of Religion in Cincinnati and Lecturer in Judaic Studies at the University of Cincinnati. He is author or editor of ten published volumes, including *Jews and Christians After the Holocaust* (1982) and *The Papers of the World Jewish Congress, 1939–1950* (2 vols., 1990; co-editor with Martin A. Cohen). He is currently writing a history of Jewish DP Camps.

Kevin A. Mahoney

On D-Day, June 6, 1944, the forces of the western Allies in "Operation Overlord"—the United States, the British Commonwealth, and France—made a successful landing on the coast of France at Normandy. Stiff German resistance contained the Allies in Normandy until late July, when a U.S. assault at St. Lô led to a breakout. The Allies then encircled and destroyed the remnant of the German army in the Falaise Pocket. Elements of General Patton's U.S. Third Army raced through Brittany; the remainder sped across France towards Germany sometimes covering 40 miles a day. On August 15, the U.S. Seventh Army and the French First Army, in Operation "Anvil-Dragoon," landed in southern France, took Marseilles, and drove north. The U.S. First Army, including a Free French division, liberated Paris on August 25.

The British and Canadians crossed into Belgium; British troops liberated Brussels in early September. Advancing through Belgium, by September 12 U.S. troops had reached the fortified German border, called the Siegfried Line or the West Wall. An attempt to reach the Rhine River through Holland by British and American forces in September ("Operation Market Garden") was unsuccessful; by October, nevertheless, elements of the U.S. First Army had crossed the Belgian border and had driven a short distance into Germany.

On the eastern front, the Soviet army launched a massive offensive in Byelorussia in late June 1944. This operation decimated Army Group Center of the German army on the eastern front. By August, Soviet forces reached Warsaw and had severely crippled the retreating German army.

From October to December 1944, U.S. troops fought from northern Belgium toward the Roer River in the northern Rhineland in an effort to reach the Rhine River. U.S. forces simultaneously advanced slowly through Alsace-Lorraine in eastern France.

On December 16, 1944, a last-ditch, all-out German offensive in Belgium's Ardennes forest of Belgium surprised the thinly-held American portion of the front in eastern Belgium and northern Luxembourg. But by early January 1945, the Allied troops in the "Battle of the Bulge" decisively halted the three attacking German armies after savage fighting. U.S. and British units counterattacked to regain lost ground, and by mid-January the Wehrmacht was falling back into Germany. At the same time, American troops stopped a German attack in Alsace-Lorraine. The Soviets also launched a large-scale offensive in January, liberating most of Poland and moving to within 40 miles of Berlin by early February.

During February 1945, the western Allies attacked on several fronts. An American assault toward the Roer River resumed, and another from eastern Belgium and northern Luxembourg continued into the Rhineland. British and Canadian forces attacked from southern Holland into Germany through the Reichswald forest. By early March, the Allies reached the Rhine. On March 7, American troops crossed the river at Remagen, the first of many crossings by American, British, Canadian, and French forces during the next month. The Allied armies sped into Germany, the British to the north toward the North Sea, and U.S. forces to the center and south, ending up in Czechoslovakia and Austria by war's end. The Soviets launched their final offensive against Berlin in April, encircling the city and meeting American troops at Torgau on the Elbe River on April 25. The Germans surrendered unconditionally to the Allies at Reims, France, on May 7. The Soviets orchestrated a second surrender ceremony in Berlin the next day, V-E Day.

In April and May of 1945, as the western Allies made their advance into Germany, some of their military units uncovered and liberated numerous concentration camps. These discoveries revealed the horror of Nazi atrocities to the western world.

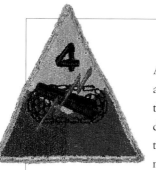

4TH ARMORED DIVISION

Arriving in Normandy in mid-July 1944, the 4th Armored Division advanced with lightning speed after the breakout of U.S. troops from the beachhead down the west coast of the Cotentin Peninsula. The division liberated the city of Avranches on July 30, then wheeled to the east racing across France. During the Battle of the Bulge—the German offensive in the Ardennes Forest that began in mid-December— the 4th engaged in fierce combat to relieve besieged American troops in the town of Bastogne, which it successfully relieved on December 27. The division renewed its offensive operations in late February, when it attacked through the Eifel Forest in the Rhineland and reached the Rhine River on March 8. Redeploying to the south, the 4th crossed the Rhine near the city of Worms and struck into central Germany. On April 4, the division liberated Ohrdruf concentration camp, a subcamp of Buchenwald, and liberated Buchenwald itself on April 11. War's end found the 4th racing into Czechoslovakia. The entire division was awarded the Distinguished Unit Citation.

89TH INFANTRY DIVISION

The 89th "Rolling W" Infantry Division made its combat debut in March 1945 as part of General George S. Patton's offensive into the Rhineland. Within a week the division had crossed both the Sauer and Moselle Rivers. On March 26, against heavy resistance, they assaulted over the Rhine. Advancing into Germany, they liberated Ohrdruf concentration camp, a subcamp of Buchenwald, on April 4. The division took the city of Eisenach two days later, rolled eastward to capture Werdau on April 17, and shortly thereafter was ordered to halt its advance. At war's end troops of the 89th were engaged in security operations.

84TH INFANTRY DIVISION

The 84th "Railsplitter" Division began its combat career in November 1944 as part of the Allied offensive toward Germany's Roer River. Advancing steadily until diverted to Belgium by the German Ardennes offensive, the 84th fought stiff defensive actions until early January, when they took the offensive to reduce the German salient. In February the Railsplitters again attacked toward Germany, crossing the Roer River on February 23. Moving into the Rhineland, the division captured the city of Krefeld on March 3. The 84th reached the Rhine on March 5, crossed it on April 1, and began a swift advance into northern Germany. The city of Hanover was seized on April 10; Hanover-Ahlem concentration camp, a subcamp of Neuengamme, was liberated the same day. Several days later the "Railsplitters" liberated Salzwedel concentration camp, another subcamp of Neuengamme, just before they reached the Elbe River.

3RD ARMORED DIVISION

Entering combat in June 1944, the 3rd "Spearhead" Armored Division fought in the Normandy hedgerows during July and seized Marigny during "Operation Cobra," the breakout from the beachhead. Executing a dramatic enveloping maneuver to close the Falaise gap and trap the German forces there, they turned eastward and reached the Reich itself by mid-September.

The division fought in the vicinity of Aachen for several months. The German onslaught in the Ardennes brought arduous combat to stop the enemy advance. Throughout January

1945, the 3rd fought to eliminate German gains, attacking into the Rhineland by February and capturing the city of Cologne in early March. Crossing the Rhine on March 23, the division helped to seal the Ruhr Pocket, in which more than 300,000 German troops surrendered; it then wheeled eastward into the Reich. On April 11, the 3rd liberated Dora-Mittelbau concentration camp, then continued their drive eastward before ceasing combat at the end of the month. The division suffered more soldiers killed in action—more than 1,800—than any other U.S. armored division in the European Theater of Operations (ETO).

6TH ARMORED DIVISION

The 6th "Super Sixth" Armored Division first met the enemy in late July 1944, during the breakout from Normandy. Swinging into Brittany, the 6th raced to the city of Brest, contained the German garrison there, then turned eastward. Attacking Alsace-Lorraine that fall, they reached the Saar River by early December. During the Battle of the Bulge, soldiers of the 6th found themselves counterattacking near the town of Bastogne against stiff resistance. Throughout the month of January, the Super Sixth fought to eliminate German forces in the Bulge. In early February the division drove through West Wall defenses; they reached the Rhine River on March 21 and crossed it several days later. Crossing the Main River near Frankfurt in early April, the 6th drove onward and liberated Buchenwald concentration camp on April 11. Continuing east, soldiers of the 6th Armored reached the Mulde River, stopping to await the approach of Soviet troops and the war's end after more than 225 days in combat.

104TH INFANTRY DIVISION

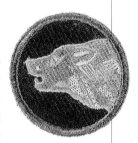

Soldiers of the 104th "Timberwolf" Infantry Division were committed to combat in October 1944 in Belgium. Reaching the Maas River in early November, the 104th assaulted the Germans near Aachen and after bitter fighting took the town of Weisweiler on November 25. Continuing their advance against stiff opposition, the Timberwolves reached the Roer River on December 13 and held defensive positions there until late February, when the 104th crossed the river to seize Düren. Continuing toward the Rhine, the Timberwolves assaulted the Erft Canal and then took the city of Cologne on March 8. Soldiers of the 104th crossed the Rhine at Honnef on March 21–22, then attacked east of the Remagen bridgehead to help reduce the Ruhr Pocket. Capturing the city of Paderborn on April 1, they later crossed the Weser and Saale Rivers. The 104th liberated Dora-Mittelbau concentration camp on April 11; after five days of heavy resistance, the division captured Halle on April 19. Their advance continued until meeting Soviet forces on April 26.

83RD INFANTRY DIVISION

In action in France soon after D-Day, the 83rd "Thunderbolt" Infantry Division was a part of the breakout near St. Lô. After moving into Brittany, the division took the port of St. Malo on August 17, then through September cleared the area along the Loire River of Germans. In Luxembourg, the 83rd defended the Moselle River, then attacked to the Siegfried Line in heavy fighting. In early December, the division moved north, attacking toward the city of Düren and the Roer River. Soldiers of the 83rd saw heavy combat in stopping the Ardennes offensive. During January 1945, they helped reduce German forces remaining in the Bulge. In early March, after a period of refitting, the 83rd attacked toward the Ruhr, reaching and crossing the Rhine near Wesel on March 29. Fighting eastward and capturing Halle on April 6, the 83rd liberated Langenstein concentration camp, a subcamp of Buchenwald, on April 11. The next day, the 83rd reached the Elbe River, where they awaited approaching Soviet forces and the war's end.

80TH INFANTRY DIVISION

The 80th "Blue Ridge" Infantry Division landed in Normandy in August 1944, first fighting to close the Falaise Gap, and liberating the town of Argentan on August 20th. Advancing toward the German border, the division fought into the Moselle region, liberating St. Avold near Saarbrücken on November 27th. After a short respite, the 80th acted to stem the German advance in Belgium. Throughout January 1945 the 80th fought to reduce German gains. In February troops of the division crossed the Our River and attacked the West Wall. Transferred south, the division plunged into the Rhineland in March, where it captured the city of Kaiserslautern on the 20th. Crossing the Rhine and Main Rivers in late March, the division advanced into central Germany, captured Gotha and Erfurt, and secured a bridgehead over the Zwick Mulde River. On April 12, the 80th liberated Buchenwald concentration camp. Joining the advance into Austria, it liberated Ebensee concentration camp, a subcamp of Mauthausen, on May 4–5.

2ND INFANTRY DIVISION

Soldiers of the 2nd "Indianhead" Infantry Division fought all of the summer of 1944 in the Normandy invasion beachhead. Pushing west into Brittany in August, the division took the fortress city of Brest. Shifting toward the German border, the division defended eastern Belgium until early December, when they moved to assault the Roer River and its vital dams. The German offensive in Belgium forced the division onto the defensive; their stubborn defense helped to stall the German advance. By the end of January, the 2nd had breached the West Wall defenses. Crossing the Roer in early March, the 2nd crossed the Rhine on the 21st. On its advance into the heart of Germany, the division captured the city of Hadamar, site of an infamous "euthanasia" facility. Having crossed the Weser River in April, the troops of the 2nd liberated Leipzig-Hasag concentration camp, a subcamp of Buchenwald, on April 14 and Spergau concentration camp three days later. After seizing Leipzig on April 19, the division advanced into Czechoslovakia, reaching Pilsen as the war ended. Troops of the 2nd spent more than 300 days in combat, suffering more than 3,000 men killed in action.

69TH INFANTRY DIVISION

The "Fighting 69th" Infantry Division first faced the Germans in February 1945 while holding a defensive position in Belgium opposite the Siegfried Line. From late February to early March, they attacked into Germany and captured the town of Dahlem. After a short rest the Fighting 69th moved to the Rhine River, crossing it on March 26–28. As the division advanced into central Germany in April, it captured—after a hard fight—the city of Weissenfels on April 14, then with the 2nd Infantry Division captured the city of Leipzig on April 19 after house-to-house fighting. That same day the 69th liberated Leipzig-Thekla, a subcamp of Buchenwald concentration camp. The division made the first contact with Soviet troops near Riesa and Torgau on the Elbe river on April 25, 1945. They remained there until the war ended.

65TH INFANTRY DIVISION

The 65th Division entered combat in early March 1945 along the Saar River. Crossing that river later in the month, the 65th captured Saarlautern after breaching the West Wall. On March 29–30, they crossed the Rhine against heavy resistance, then captured the town of Langensalza on April 6. The 65th liberated a subcamp of Flossenbürg concentration camp on April 20–21. Two days later, the division took the city of Neumarkt. The 65th crossed the Danube River on April 26 and seized the industrial city of Regensburg the following day. Early May found the division in Austria, where they occupied the city of Linz just before war's end.

90TH INFANTRY DIVISION

A regiment of the 90th "Tough Ombre" Infantry Division landed in France on D-Day, June 6, 1944. After much combat in the beachhead, the 90th helped to close the Falaise Gap in August. They then pursued the defeated Germans toward the Reich, besieging the fortress town of Metz in eastern France that fall. In December the division advanced into the Saar, but the German Ardennes offensive in Belgium placed it on the defensive. In January 1945, the 90th was moved to Belgium to re-take ground lost to the Germans. February saw the division again advancing, now through the Siegfried Line into the Rhineland, where it captured the German city of Mainz on March 22. Crossing the Rhine two days later, the division liberated Flossenbürg concentration camp in Bavaria on April 23, 1945. For the 90th, the war ended in Czechoslovakia after they had spent more days in combat than any other division in the European Theater.

10TH ARMORED DIVISION

The 10th Armored "Tiger" Division landed in France in late September 1944 and entered combat that November in eastern France. It went on the offensive that month, crossing the Moselle River and driving to the Saar River. The mid-December German attack in Belgium brought the division to battle, fighting to maintain contact with the just relieved town of Bastogne. In early January, the 10th moved to defensive positions. By late February the division was on the attack again in the Saar-Moselle region, driving toward Saarburg and capturing Trier on March 15. The division crossed the Rhine River on March 28 near Mannheim, then turned south. The 10th liberated Landsberg concentration camp on April 27 and ended the war at Innsbruck, Austria.

12TH ARMORED DIVISION

The Twelfth "Hellcat" Armored Division began its combat career in the Vosges Mountains of eastern France in early December 1944. Withdrawn for refitting after a month of attacking, the "Hellcats" resumed the offensive in early January, meeting stiff resistance from German defenders until early February, when they joined with French forces to seal the Colmar pocket in Alsace. Mid-March found the 12th advancing into the Rhineland; it reached the Rhine on March 20. Capturing the city of Ludwigshafen on March 21, soldiers of the division crossed the Rhine on March 28–29 and began their swift advance into Bavaria. The 12th captured Würzburg in early April and reached the Danube River on April 22. The division liberated Landsberg concentration camp, a subcamp of Dachau, on April 27 as it sped south toward Austria, where it ended the war.

103RD INFANTRY DIVISION

The 103rd "Cactus" Infantry Division first faced the Germans in the French Vosges in early November 1944. Attacking toward the border of the Reich, soldiers of the division crossed into Germany on December 14. On the defensive during the Ardennes offensive, by mid-January the 103rd was helping to stop another German offensive in Alsace-Lorraine. By mid-March the Cactus division was again on the offensive, blasting through the Siegfried Line into the Rhineland and consolidating positions on the western side of the Rhine. Moving into Bavaria, the 103rd forestalled the escape of German forces from Stuttgart, then crossed the Danube on April 26. The next day soldiers of the 103rd liberated Landsberg concentration camp, a subcamp of Dachau. Moving into Austria, the Cactus division accepted the surrender of the city of Innsbruck on May 4 and met American troops advancing from Italy.

4TH INFANTRY DIVISION

The 4th "Ivy" Infantry Division landed at Utah Beach on D-Day, June 6, 1944. The division quickly moved up the Cotentin Peninsula to besiege and liberate Cherbourg. Engaged in hard combat during that summer, the 4th helped to halt a German counteroffensive at Mortain in early August, then pursued the defeated Germans, liberating Paris on August 25. That fall the division was engaged in the bloody fighting in the Hürtgen forest as the Allies attempted to crack the Siegfried Line. In December the Ivy Division defended the southern edge of the German advance in the Ardennes, then advanced to reduce German forces in January. The division moved into the Rhineland in early February, breaching the West Wall in heavy fighting. After moving through the Rhineland, soldiers of the 4th crossed the Rhine River by the end of March, captured the city of Nuremberg on April 17, and continued into Bavaria. On April 28–29, the 4th Infantry Division liberated a sub-camp of Dachau in Bavaria. At the war's end, the division was located at Berchtesgaden, Hitler's mountain retreat. The Ivy Division suffered more men killed in action from D-Day to war's end than any other U.S. division serving in the European Theater of Operations.

20TH ARMORED DIVISION

The 20th Armored Division arrived in Germany in early April 1945. Committed to combat in late April, they spearheaded the drive on Munich at the end of the month. The 20th was one of the divisions that liberated Dachau concentration camp on April 29. After a hard fight for Munich, in early May the division crossed into Austria, where it remained until the war's end.

42ND INFANTRY DIVISION

Elements of the 42nd "Rainbow" Infantry Division faced the Germans for the first time on December 24, 1944, near Strasbourg. After holding against a German offensive in Alsace-Lorraine in January, the entire division entered combat in mid-February and took up defensive positions in the Hardt Mountains of Alsace. In mid-March, the division went on the attack and broke through the West Wall into Germany. Crossing the Rhine on March 31, the 42nd captured Würzburg in early April, followed by Schweinfurt and Fürth. Speeding south, the Rainbow Division was one of the divisions that liberated Dachau concentration camp on April 29. Having passed through Munich, the division ended the war in Austria in early May.

45TH INFANTRY DIVISION

The 45th "Thunderbird" Infantry Division landed in Sicily in July 1943 and then assaulted the beaches of Salerno that September. After crossing the Volturno River, they battled up the Italian peninsula until being withdrawn for the late-January landing at Anzio. The 45th was in continuous action until May, when they broke out from the beachhead, then raced to outflank Rome. The Thunderbirds went ashore with the invasion of southern France on August 15, 1944, and drove north up the Rhone River valley, where they liberated Epinal on September 25. Advancing into the Vosges Mountains, the division fought in eastern France during the next few months. Withdrawn for a short respite from combat during February 1945, the 45th returned to action in March, crossing the Rhine near Hamm on March 26. Moving swiftly into southern Germany, the Thunderbirds captured Nuremberg on April 20. While driving for Munich, the division liberated Dachau concentration camp on April 29.

14TH ARMORED DIVISION

The 14th Armored Division landed in southern France in October 1944 and entered combat in late November as part of the Allied drive to clear the Vosges Mountains in eastern France. Continuing to advance toward the German border in December, it was hit by several German counterattacks in Alsace-Lorraine in January 1945; the enemy was thwarted, in part, by the division's stubborn resistance. After a period of rehabilitation, the 14th returned to  the offensive in mid-March, crossing the Moder River, breaching the Siegfried Line, and racing to the Rhine at Germersheim by March 23. Striking swiftly into Bavaria, the 14th captured Neustadt, then continued through the heart of southern Germany to reach the Danube in late April. On May 3, the division liberated subcamps of Dachau concentration camp, then plunged into Austria, where it ended the war a few days later.

8TH INFANTRY DIVISION

The 8th "Arrow" Infantry Division began its World War II combat career in early July 1944 in Normandy. Advancing out of the beachhead in early August, the division liberated the city of Rennes, then moved into Brittany and attacked the city of Brest. By November the division was in action on the border of the Reich, joining the fierce fighting for the Hürtgen Forest, which it seized in November. The 8th continued to advance eastward toward the Roer River during December. Troops of the division crossed the Roer at the end of February, then pushed to the Rhine River near Cologne in early March. The 8th was involved in the reduction of the Ruhr Pocket, forming one jaw of the pincers which sealed the pocket on April 17. By the end of the month, under British command, the division helped to establish a bridgehead across the Elbe River. They liberated the Wöbbelin concentration camp, a subcamp of Neuengamme, on May 3, shortly before hostilities ceased.

82ND AIRBORNE DIVISION

The "All American" 82nd Airborne Division parachuted into Sicily in July 1943, then made an airborne landing at Salerno in September to spearhead the invasion of Italy. Their next combat jump was early on June 6, 1944, in support of the Normandy invasion; they fought

in the beachhead for the next month. After a return to England, the "All Americans" landed at Nijmegen in September as part of an Allied attempt to drive into Germany through the Netherlands. Fighting there until early November, the "All Americans" returned to combat that December to help stem the German onslaught in the Ardennes. The 82nd helped eliminate German gains, then advanced through the West Wall to cross the Roer River in mid-February. Early April found the 82nd on the Rhine, securing the city of Cologne. The division then moved into central Germany and crossed the Elbe River on April 30. Wöbbelin concentration camp, a subcamp of Neuengamme, was liberated by the division on May 3. At war's end the 82nd was part of an Allied occupation force in Berlin.

99TH INFANTRY DIVISION

The 99th Infantry Division was initially assigned to defensive positions in eastern Belgium in late 1944, but it soon joined the U.S. attack toward the Roer River. The German Ardennes Offensive, however, hit the division hard. Although partly surrounded, the 99th held new defensive positions until the end of January, when they counterattacked into the Monschau Forest. Withdrawn for rehabilitation, the 99th returned to action in early March and attacked into the Rhineland. Troops of the division crossed the Rhine at Remagen on March 11, then fought to expand the bridgehead. After seizing Giessen on March 29, the division helped reduce the Ruhr pocket until mid-April. Moving into Bavaria, the 99th crossed the Ludwig Canal against stiff resistance and established a bridgehead over the Alt river on April 25. Pushing farther into Bavaria, the troops of the 99th liberated a subcamp of Dachau concentration camp May 3–4, and ended the war at the Inn River in southern Bavaria.

11TH ARMORED DIVISION

The 11th Armored "Thunderbolt" Division first fought in late December 1944 during the Battle of the Bulge. Immediately engaged in fierce combat, they counterattacked German forces near Bastogne. Continuing to attack throughout January, the Thunderbolters helped eliminate German gains by joining with other American units to seal German forces in the Bulge. Early February found the 11th attacking against heavy resistance through the Siegfried Line. The division reached the Rhine in early March. After a short rest, the 11th was redeployed and again reached the Rhine, entering the city of Worms on March 21. In early April, troopers of the 11th advanced into central Germany, where they captured the city of Coburg on April 11 and Bayreuth several days later. Resuming their lightning advance into Austria, they took the city of Linz on May 5. The Thunderbolt Division liberated Gusen concentration camp, a subcamp of Mauthausen, also on May 5, and the Mauthausen camp itself on May 6. Soon after, the 11th met Soviet forces.

71ST INFANTRY DIVISION

Committed to action in Alsace-Lorraine on March 11, 1945, the 71st Infantry division penetrated the Siegfried Line a few days later. Soldiers of the division then captured the town of Pirmasens and crossed the Rhine near Oppenheim at the end of the month. Advancing into south-central Germany, troops of the division captured the city of Bayreuth April 14–16 after heavy combat. Moving swiftly south, the division reached the Danube on April 26 and captured the city of Regensburg the next day. Crossing the Austrian border on May 2, the 71st reached the city of Steyr by May 5. On May 5–6, troops of the division liberated Gunskirchen concentration camp, a subcamp of Mauthausen. The division remained in Austria as the war ended a few days later.

9TH ARMORED DIVISION

The 9th Armored Division, after landing in France in early October 1944, was initially assigned to a quiet front in Luxembourg. The German offensive in mid-December struck the division squarely and the 9th responded with fierce delaying actions in several towns. Part of the division helped to hold the vital town of Bastogne. Following a withdrawal for refitting and rehabilitation, the 9th again entered combat in late February and crossed the Roer River. Reaching the Rhine on March 7, the 9th captured the Ludendorf Bridge at Remagen intact and crossed the river the same day. As it drove into central Germany, the division captured the city of Limburg, then continued on to hold a line along the Mulde River in mid-April. At the end of the month the 9th shifted south and drove into Czechoslovakia where, on May 7, it liberated Falkenau a.d. Eger, a subcamp of Flossenbürg, just as hostilities ended.

1ST INFANTRY DIVISION

The 1st "The Red One" Infantry Division, the oldest division in the U.S. Army, landed in North Africa in November 1942 and fought in Tunisia until Axis forces were defeated there in May 1943. That July, the division then assaulted the island of Sicily. Returning to combat on D-Day, June 6, 1944, troops of the 1st landed on bloody Omaha Beach, fighting among the Normandy hedgerows until they drove out of the beachhead and joined the pursuit of the defeated Germans to the borders of the Reich. After capturing the city of Aachen in October, the 1st then battled through the infamous Hürtgen Forest into the Siegfried Line. The German Ardennes Offensive found the division fighting to stem the German advance in Belgium; they counterattacked into Germany and, by the end of February 1945, had crossed the Roer River, capturing the city of Bonn on March 9. Crossing the Rhine on March 15, soldiers of the 1st helped to encircle the Ruhr Pocket. As the division advanced into the heart of Germany, on May 7 its troops liberated Falkenau a.d. Eger concentration camp, a subcamp of Flossenbürg.

ALLIED UNITS

SOVIET 60TH ARMY

The Soviet 60th Army was formed in the summer of 1942 and committed to action in January 1943 near Voronezh as part of a Soviet winter offensive. The following summer, the army fought as part of the Soviet forces that defeated the German army at the battle of Kursk in July. Starting on the long road to Berlin that summer, units of the 60th helped to liberate Kiev later in the year. They advanced into Poland as part of the great Soviet offensive in the summer of 1944. On January 27, 1945, units of the 60th Army liberated the Auschwitz concentration camp complex in western Poland. Driving into the Reich, the 60th Army finished the war in Czechoslovakia.

2ND CANADIAN DIVISION

The 2nd Canadian Division first battled the Germans on the coast of France in August 1942 during the raid on Dieppe, the "dress rehearsal" for the invasion of the continent. Landing in France in July 1944, the division fought to liberate Caen and then helped to encircle the remnants of the German army in Normandy at the Falaise Gap. During the pursuit of the defeated enemy toward the Reich, the Canadians liberated Dieppe, then helped clear the Scheldt River estuary to open the port of Antwerp for the Allies. After wintering in defensive positions in Holland, the Canadians fought through the Reichswald forest toward the Rhine. They crossed the river on March 28 and spearheaded the Commonwealth drive toward the North Sea. While clearing eastern Holland of German forces, they liberated Westerbork Transit Camp on April 12. Continuing their advance into northern Germany, the division reached Oldenburg by war's end.

BRITISH 11TH ARMORED DIVISION

The 11th Armored Division landed in Normandy soon after the invasion, taking part in the hard fighting in the Normandy beachhead and the breakout in August. Pursing the defeated German forces the division liberated the port of Antwerp, Belgium, in early September. Later that month it supported "Operation Market Garden," the British airborne drive into Holland. Continuing their operations in the southern Netherlands that fall, they held defensive positions along the Maas River through the winter. The 11th was part of the British offensive toward the Rhine during February and March, fighting through the Reichswald forest with the Canadians. Crossing the Rhine in late March, the division secured a bridgehead over the Aller River and liberated the Bergen-Belsen concentration camp on April 15. By the end of the month they had crossed the Elbe River and captured the Baltic port of Lübeck shortly before the war ended.

1ST POLISH ARMY

The 1st Polish Army was formed in spring 1944 from Polish units created the previous year by the Soviet-sponsored Union of Polish Patriots. Entering combat in the summer of 1944, it reached the suburbs of Warsaw in August. The failure of the Soviet attempt to take Warsaw, including a valiant attempt by Polish troops to cross the Vistula and aid the Home Army insurrection in Warsaw, left the Poles in defensive positions opposite their capital for the remainder of the year. In January 1945 troops of the 1st Army helped liberate Warsaw, then pushed on toward the Baltic Sea, where they seized the city of Kolberg in mid-March. In the next month the Poles joined the final attack on Berlin, moving north of the city; units of the army helped encircle Berlin. They liber- ated Sachsenhausen concentration camp on April 22 and reached the Elbe River as the war came to an end.

NOTE

These American divisions have been certified as liberators of concentration camps by the U.S. Army's Center for Military History as of April 1, 1995. The Center defines a liberating division as one whose official military documents prove its presence at a camp within 48 hours of the first soldier's arrival. The divisions are listed chronologically by camp liberation dates.

SOURCES

Conner, Albert Z. and Robert G. Poirier. *Red Army Order of Battle in the Great Patriotic War*. Novato, CA, 1985.

Ellis, L. F. *Victory in the West*. 2 vols. London, 1962 & 1968.

Garlinski, Jósef. *Poland in the Second World War*. New York, 1985.

Joslen, H. F. *Orders of Battle, Second World War, 1939–1945*. London, 1960.

Pospelov, Petr N., ed. *Istoriia Velikoi Otechestvennoi Voiny Sovetskogo Soiuza*. Vols. 4–5. Moscow, 1963–64.

Stanton, Shelby. *Order of Battle: U.S. Army of World War II*. Novato, CA, 1984.

U.S. Army, Historical Division. *Combat Chronicle: An Outline History of U.S. Army Divisions*. Washington, D.C., 1946.

U.S. Army, Office of Theater History, European Theater. *Order of Battle of the United States Army World War II: European Theater of Operations, Divisions*. Paris, 1945.

KEVIN MAHONEY is a consultant to the U.S. Holocaust Memorial Museum. He was a researcher on several volumes in the *The Third Reich* series (Time-Life Books), primary researcher for *Darkness Before Dawn* (USHMM, 1994) and general editor of *1945: The Year of Liberation* (USHMM, 1995).

ON LIBERATION OF THE CAMPS

Abzug, Robert H. *Inside the Vicious Heart: Americans and the Liberation of Nazi Concentration Camps.* New York: Oxford University Press, 1985.

Bridgman, Jon. *The End of the Holocaust: The Liberation of the Camps.* Portland, OR: Areopagitica Press, 1990.

Chamberlin, Brewster and Marcia Feldman. *The Liberation of the Nazi Concentration Camps 1945.* Washington, D.C.: United States Holocaust Memorial Council, 1987.

Sington, Derrick. *Belsen Uncovered.* London: Duckworth, 1946.

Smith, Marcus, *The Harrowing of Hell: Dachau.* Albuquerque: University of New Mexico Press, 1972; reprint, Albany, NY: State University of New York Press, 1995.

ON CONFRONTING ATROCITIES

Bourke-White, Margaret. *"Dear Fatherland, Rest Quietly": A Report on the Collapse of Hitler's "Thousand Years."* New York: Simon and Schuster, 1946.

Penrose, Anthony, ed. *Lee Miller's War: Photographer and Correspondent with the Allies in Europe, 1944–1945.* Boston, Toronto, and London: Little, Brown, and Co., Bullfinch Press, 1992.

Pronay, Nicholas, and Keith Wilson, eds. *The Political Re-education of Germany and Her Allies.* Totowa, NJ: Barnes and Noble Books, 1985.

Roeder, George H., Jr. *The Censored War: American Visual Experience during World War Two.* New Haven: Yale University Press, 1993.

ON EARLY WAR CRIMES TRIALS

Conot, Robert E. *Justice at Nuremberg.* New York: Harper & Row, 1983.

Davidson, Eugene. *The Trial of the Germans: An Account of the Twenty-two Defendants before the International Military Tribunal at Nuremberg.* New York: Macmillan, 1966.

Taylor, Telford. *The Anatomy of the Nuremberg Trials: A Personal Memoir.* New York: Knopf, 1992.

ON A CONTINENT IN CHAOS: EUROPE AND THE DISPLACED PERSONS

Dinnerstein, Leonard. *America and the Survivors of the Holocaust.* New York: Columbia University Press, 1982.

Peck, Abraham J., ed. *The Landsberg DP Camp Letters of Major Irving Heymont, United States Army.* Cincinnati: American Jewish Archives, 1982.

Proudfoot, Malcolm J. *European Refugees, 1939–52: A Study in Forced Population Movement.* Evanston, IL: Northwestern University Press, 1956.

Schwarz, Leo. *The Redeemers: A Saga of the Years 1945–1952.* New York: Farrar, Straus, and Young, 1953.

Wyman, Mark. *DP: Europe's Displaced Persons, 1945–1951.* Philadelphia: The Balch Institute Press, 1989.